I0004358

How To Build a BRILLIANT Business With The Internet:

101 essential hints & tips for every successful small business and entrepreneur

Linda Parkinson-Hardman

© 2008, Linda Parkinson-Hardman

All rights reserved. The right of Linda Parkinson-Hardman to be identified as the author of this work has been asserted by her in accordance with the Copyright, Designs and Patents Act 1988.

No paragraph of this publication may be reproduced, copied or transmitted save with written permission or in accordance with the provisions of the Copyright, Designs and Patents Act 1988, or under the terms of any license, permitting limited copying issued by the Copyright Licensing Agency, 33 Alfred Place, London, WC1E 7DP.

Any person who does any unauthorised act in relation to this publication may be liable to criminal prosecution and civil claims for damages.

British Library Cataloguing In Publication Data
A Catalogue record for this book is available from The British Library.

ISBN Number: 978-0-9556906-0-0

First edition published by:
Crystal Clear Books
The Gables, Acreman Close
Cerne Abbas
Dorchester
Dorset, DT2 7JU

Telephone: 0870 3301267
website: www.crystalclearbooks.co.uk

Note/Disclaimer: The material contained in this book is set out in good faith for general guidance and no liability can be accepted for loss of expense incurred as a result of relying in particular circumstances on a statement made in the book. The laws and regulations are complex and liable to change without notice and readers should check the current position with the relevant authorities before making personal arrangements.

This book is dedicated to the memory of Alf Caswell,
my dad, without whom it wouldn't have been possible
as he always encouraged me to go the extra mile!

Contents

Introduction

It all started with a question! The question was the subject of discussion amongst a group of friends and myself who were wasting a sunny, summer afternoon in 2005 drinking coffee and chatting. The question became a turning a point for all of us and everyone is now travelling down a different road to the one we were on before that day.

And the question? Well the question was *'how can you persuade 100,000 people to give you £1 each?'*. The discussions were wide ranging and covered the sensible (not profitable enough), the wacky (who on earth is going to pay for 'that') to the seriously dodgy (I don't even think some of them are legal!). But, having said all that, I realised that I had the makings of a book; not because of the discussion, interesting though it was, but because I have been running online businesses since 1996 and realised that I actually knew a lot more about how to make the Internet work hard to grow a business than many others.

This then is a book of dreams, the dreams you have for your life, your business and your future. I started down the road of using the Internet to develop my business because I had a dream of a better lifestyle; so that I could avoid the office politics I was plagued with, and in order to have a more normal work/life balance. This isn't a book about how to make a million overnight though, it is simply a book that will help you to help your business grow using one of the most innovative mediums to have been developed in the modern age - the Internet.   It takes the form of easily digestible chunks of information covering a whole range of subjects, from websites (and whether you need one or not), through the legal flotsam and jetsom and right into online marketing. Everything I talk about is something I have used along the way to make my business more successful. The tools and techniques I discuss are, more often that not, free or low cost.

For those of you who would like a little more hand holding, I also offer mentoring and a series of innovative workshops that take place in the beautiful county of Dorset; more information about all the work I do can be found at *growabetterbusiness.co.uk*.

So I'll just say good luck, enjoy the reading and when you have made that first £100,000 let me know and I will gladly celebrate with you!

Linda

In The Beginning Was The Business Plan

Jerry just loved sending email!
© Photographer: Dejan Savic | Agency: Dreamstime.com

You may remember the late 1990's and the dot.com boom... and then bust, as big name after big name went out of business. At the time, the hype was all about something called e-commerce, which was going to re-write the way in which the world did business.

Then suddenly it was gone and we rarely hear the word e-commerce these days, so much so, that it could look like it had died and gone to Internet heaven, never to be seen again (just like some of the emails that we send which never seem to appear). But you'd be wrong, e-commerce isn't dead, it has just changed into 'commerce'.

The pundits of the 1990's were right, the Internet did change the way in which we all do business, just not in the way they expected it to. Now it is so ingrained in our culture that we no longer need special words to define it as something special. In fact e-commerce is very much alive and kicking, and you are about to become a part of that revolution.

1. Sustainable business

The word sustainable is seen everywhere these days, in farming, the environmental movement and now even in business. But just what is a sustainable business? Well, as far as I am concerned, it is one that meets the needs of both it's owners/employees and it's customers. It is one that can cope with the volume of sales or visitors that it gets and can even grow without using too many of the worlds resources to help it do so.

Which, of course, is where the Internet comes in - no longer do we need to have expensive shops with all that electricity being wasted in lighting the place, nor do we need the endless numbers of plastic carriers to carry what we produce. We don't need cars to travel to the shop, we simply login and away we go.

But can it really be that simple? The above statement is, I know, very simplistic and there are many shades of grey to be taken into account, including packing materials for items posted, the overstretched postal delivery services and the resultant eyestrain from too many hours spent online. However, all in all, I do feel that the Internet pays it's way well and it certainly enables businesses to do far more than they would be able to do in the 'real' world.

As this could be an ongoing debate I'd love to get your thoughts on the matter too - so email me and I'll add the most interesting comments to the website, alternatively you can add a comment yourself at ***growabetterbusiness.co.uk***.

2. What's your motivation?

To succeed in any business you need to have a very clear idea about what your motivation for being in business is. Many of us might say, "well, I'd just like to make shed loads of cash please", but there is often something else as well, such as spending more time with the family, being able to go white water rafting whenever you please or just having more 'me time'.

You may even be motivated to change the world in some way; this is often the case when great entrepreneurs are driven by a purpose that is usually bigger than money. They may have started out needing to make a few bucks at the beginning, but it morphed into something else entirely.

You may want to make it easier to use technology, provide a much needed service or give information where there wasn't any before, improve a process or a product or even enable customers to buy something more easily.

Discovering what your real motivation is could be half the battle in making it work for the people that matter most, your customers.

3. Could you make it an interest or hobby?

What is your business about? Is it going to be an extension of an interest or hobby you already have, have you worked in a similar area before, or are you starting on something completely new to you? Whatever your plan, you must know what you are doing or you may find yourself coming unstuck.

Most people start a business because they either have a passion for something or to do something they already do, better than it is currently being done. In both of these cases, they know what they are about and they have some experience of the area they want to work in already. It would be foolish to attempt to start an Internet bookshop if you didn't know anything about the way in which the bookselling (and to some extent the book publishing) industry works.

So, if you do want to do something in an area you think you might like, but know nothing about see if there is anywhere you could you go for help, advice or even training? For instance, going back to that Internet bookshop - you might get a part-time job with a local bookseller to see the mechanics of how it all works. Alternatively, you might find an online community that could tell you what's what or even find a mentor of some description.

Whatever you decide to do, get some experience before you begin otherwise you will have a very steep learning curve. It helps to be passionate about your business too because doing the accounts at 2.00am isn't much fun if you aren't enjoying what you do!

4. The only ways you can make money

First, let's get one thing straight and lay to rest a few myths at the same time. Ultimately, there are only two ways to make money on the Internet (or in the real world for that matter).

The first, and possibly the easiest, is to sell something that other people have provided you with, whether it is new parts for cars, second-hand books or an advertising service for other businesses.

The second way to make money, which is possibly the most profitable albeit more difficult, is to sell something you make yourself. It could be model airplanes, designer cushions or the book you wrote yesterday!

Having said all that, there are many shades of grey for each of these methods and that, dear readers, is the purpose of this book.

5. Selling other peoples stuff

The easiest way to make money, *'any place, any time, anywhere'*, is to sell something that someone else has provided you with. In the case of your local high street shop this is usually referred to as 'stock', and stock is everything that you buy from one place (usually a wholesaler) to sell somewhere else at a higher price. The difference between the price you paid for your stock and what your customers pay is your profit. It is out of this profit that all of your other costs will have to be met. Now, I'm going to assume that you have never run any sort of a business before, but if you have then you may like to skip the rest of this hint and move along quickly to the next.

Let's assume that you have a little shop on the corner next to the grocers. You sell books for £5 each. You get the books from your supplier for £3 each, and the £2 difference is your profit. Now, lets assume that you are renting your shop for £100 per month (rent is an outgoing expense), this immediately means that you will need to sell at least 50 books each month just to cover the rent on the shop.

Let's add other items to your expenses like electricity for your heating and lighting; these might come in at around £30 each per month. Remember, every time you do something extra, you will have a cost added to your outgoing expenses, and we haven't even started on what you want to earn yourself yet (but we will assume you want to make £100 a week: that's not unreasonable is it?)

So the costs for one month might look like this:

- Electricity £30.00
- Gas £30.00
- Rent £100.00
- Wages £400.00

So far your total costs are £560 and to cover those costs you will have to sell 280 books (£560 divided by £2 profit). But those books also cost money to buy that we haven't factored in yet (it adds another £840 on your costs). Therefore, to cover the first month you will actually need to make £1400 and happily, selling 280 books at £5 each means that you make £1400. Congratulations, you have just broken even!

Breaking the above down even further means that you will need to sell a minimum of ten books each day (assuming you open seven days a week) to cover all of these costs.

I know you are now thinking what is the point of all that, *"I'm planning to make my millions on the Internet and I don't have to worry about rent on a shop"*. The problem is that you will still have costs that need to be taken into account and your stock, if you choose to sell something that someone else is providing, will be your biggest single outlay.

You don't necessarily have to sell physical items in order to make money with 'stock' though, especially on the Internet. You could make money through what are called affiliate schemes, which is where you create adverts that link to someone's product who will then pay you a small sum every time someone buys. You could also make a few pounds by selling advertising space on a website of your own. However, these are all versions of 'someone else's products' and you need to make time to find the best ones to promote and how to market them in just the same way as the person running the bookstore does.

6. Selling your own stuff

This is a much harder way to make your money, whether you sell online or in the little shop next to the grocers, because you actually have to produce the item/s first. However, it is potentially the most profitable because you don't have to share any of the profits with wholesalers if you prefer not to.

If you are making designer cushions, then you will need a sewing machine (fixed asset), materials, thread, stuffing and ribbons or other embellishments at the very least, as well as a whole lot of working space. You will need to have an idea of how long it takes you to make one cushion, because this will tell you how many you can make in a week, which in turn tells you how many you can sell in a week. Therefore, if you can only make ten a week, you will need to charge more for them than if you could make 20, 30, 60 or 100. These figures will also determine what the selling price of each cushion will be which, in turn, determines whether your chosen market is going to be able to afford them.

You will also find out whether you can ever take a holiday again, because you will need to build up enough stock to carry you through your week in Bognor Regis when you won't be making any cushions at all. Unless of course you're like me and take your work on holiday with you (part of this book was written whilst on 'holiday' in Malta and Cyprus!).

If you are creating music, software or images you may not have any direct costs to worry about because they are often sold as digital downloads from a website or myspace page. Nevertheless, you will still have to factor in your time and therefore you have the same issues as the person making the designer cushions. How many tracks can you create in one week? Most music downloads sell for around 79p, so to make £100 each week, you will need to sell one track at least 127 times or, to put it another way, 127 different tracks once each.

7. How much do you want to spend?

OK, so you have decided you are going to set up a small business, running it from home - how hard can it be I hear you ask. 'I'll just get a few things and I'll stick them on Ebay and the money will start rolling in'. It can seem very simple when you put it like that but you need to be aware of just what it may cost you in money, and time, before you even start. In other words, this question might more appropriately be 'how much can you afford to lose'!

A few questions you might like to think about are:

- How much time do you want to spend working on this new business? Just an hour or so each week/month or are you prepared to spend a couple of hours a day on it?
- How much money do you have to invest in your stock or do you have something of your own you could sell: books or craft items for example?
- If you are making items, or writing a book, how much time do you need to make or develop each them?
- Will you charge your customers post and packing costs, and if so how are you calculating them?
- How will you go about shipping your products to your customers and can you get to a post office easily to send orders?
- How much money can you afford to lose if it doesn't work as you will need to make some investments in things like stock, materials, a website and marketing?

- What do your family and friends think about your ideas? Are they willing to help packing orders, posting them or helping with the manufacture for example.

All of these questions need to be answered as honestly as possible; there is no point in saying you are willing to work for a couple of hours everyday if you work full-time already, have a family that needs to be ferried about and half a dozen hobbies you enjoy. Your new business, instead of being a pleasure, will become just another pressure that adds to the many others you are currently juggling. On the other hand, you may be retired or work part-time and can easily fit it in.

Remember as well, that your business will not be just about taking orders, packing them up and then going to the post office. You will also need to factor in time to answer the 'phone, reply to emails, create invoices, do the filing and 101 other administrative tasks that don't actually bring in any money themselves, but are essential if you are going to deliver a quality service to your customers.

Being realistic at the front end will save many hassles and headaches further down the road, and if your business takes off in an unexpected way, then you can look at ways of re-arranging your time, and resources, to help it grow even more.

8. A little business planning goes a long way

If you want to start a business then you will need some sort of business plan; it doesn't have to be huge or overly complicated, but as my husband is very fond of saying "if you don't know where you're going, any road will take you there". In other words, if you don't have an idea of where you would like to be (with your business) in say, twelve months then how will you know if it's successful?

A reasonable business plan should include a number of basic elements, which describe:

- why you are in business, what you are selling and why you think it will work
- a brief description of your market and your customers needs and expectations
- some explanation as to why they will buy from you
- some information about your competitors
- what makes you different from other companies providing the same product or service (this is known as your *unique selling point*)
- a cash flow forecast covering 6, 12, 18 and 24 months
- a sales forecast covering your first two years in business
- your marketing strategy
- a 'baby-bio'/track record about you, and one for each of the people working with you, describing who you are, what your background is and your skills/abilities (this is particularly important if you are hoping to raise some finance from the bank).

Not all of these elements will be necessary if you are just planning to sell the odd item on Ebay every month or so. In these circumstances, a brief idea of how much money you would like to make and what your costs are going to be will probably be more than enough to convince you whether it is the right thing to do. However, if you are intending to do something more structured and formal, then you will need all of the sections to be completed - but don't panic, there are hints and tips here to help you work out what needs to go into each one.

9. Who is your target market?

Identifying your target market will go a long way to defining how much, and how little, you can sell to whom and in what way. For instance, you might be selling children's clothes, but your target market is not children, indeed it is their parents because they have the purchasing power. On the other hand it is worth bearing in mind that lots of supermarkets have been criticised over the years for targeting the 'pester power' of children, who then put a great deal of pressure on their parents to buy sweets or toys for them. These sorts of campaigns work because they create a demand amongst children which is based on peer pressure; in other words if a friend has one, I want one too.

Whilst it is unlikely that you will be targeting this sort of market, at least not in the first few days, you do need to think about who your product will appeal to and who will be the buyer, because they are not necessarily the same person. Take flowers for instance, they may appeal to women, but may well be bought be men.

I would like to suggest that you spend a few minutes just writing down on your business plan template what your product is, who will want it, why they will want it and who is most likely to buy it.

10. Who are your competitors?

You can be sure that you will not be entering this business arena alone, unless you have a completely new and innovative product that no one has ever thought of before. If this isn't the case then getting to know your competitors is always a good idea because they will help you (albeit unknowingly) to build a better business.

Have a look for the competition; maybe they have a shop? Do they have a web presence as well? If you are planning to sell greeting cards for instance then your competitors will be on the local high street, they may be online retailers and could even be small-scale ebay sellers. Have a look at how they present themselves, can you tell what section of the market they are hoping to attract? Try them out, look at their marketing material, and find out about their sales process and how they interact with potential customers. What do they say about themselves and can you tell how successful they are?

By answering these questions, you will start to get a feel for what might, or might not work. As a result, you will be able to improve on what they are offering. Just a word to the wise though, your competitors (if they are any good) will be doing this to you too!

11. Cash flow and profitability

Businesses can fail, even large corporations, if they don't get the cash flow (money they can get their hands on immediately) right. It doesn't matter what the business is worth, if there is not enough cash to sustain the day-to-day running costs the end is predictable. So what is 'cash flow', why is it different to 'profitability' and does it really matter?

Cash really is king when it comes to business; it is what oils the wheels of commerce and it certainly helps when you have bills to pay. A business operates based on money coming in (preferably from lots of sales) and money going out (for things like stock). The best way to operate would be to have cash arriving in your bank account immediately an order is placed and then not having to pay your bills until the very last minute.

So, at its simplest, cash flow management means delaying outlays of cash as long as you can whilst encouraging anyone who owes you money to pay it as rapidly as possible.

It could pay to have a look at your projected cash flow over the coming twelve months, particularly if you are planning to have any regular payments such as office rental charges. This must be as realistic as you can make it because it is this tool that will tell you whether you can afford to eat next month!

To create a cash flow forecast you simply need to subtract all your monthly outgoings (the money you expect to pay to someone else) from your expected monthly income (the money that people pay you). Each time you reach a monthly total, whether it is on the plus or the negative side, you roll it over to the next month and start again - you can see a very simple example below.

	Jan	Feb	Mar	Apr	May	June
Carry Forward	0.00	-50.00	-60.00	-20.00	10.00	70.00
Income	100	110	120	130	140	150
Expenditure	150	120	80	100	80	100
Total	-50.00	-60.00	-20.00	10.00	70.00	120.00

12. Seven simple ways to improve cash flow

- If you have a bill to pay and it says 30 days, don't pay it on day 15 - you are paying too early (don't forget however, that everyone else is going to want to do this to you as well if they can!).

- If you have made a sale, get the payment as soon as you can. If you are selling tangible goods such as books then ask for payment immediately, by credit card, cheque, or cash.

- Depending on the business you are in, you may prefer not to send out any goods until payment has been made.

- If you are doing freelance work, ensure that your contract states payment on completion, *before* you hand over the software or the images.

- Take as little cash for yourself out of your business as you can reasonably afford initially - the less cash you have in your business, the harder it may be to pay the people you owe money to, such as your suppliers.

- Avoid being overdrawn at the bank, unless it is pre-arranged; the charges will be high and you will be paying them out of your hard earned profits.

- If you are selling services then ensure you have a deposit payment up front, this should be enough to cover all your initial costs, such as materials and labour. You may also want to set up stage payments if it is a long or complex job.

Business In Action

George was pleased to have picked up his very own
organic manure machine so cheaply!
© Photographer: Dejan Savic | Agency: Dreamstime.com

Sometimes, being in business can feel a little like pushing a very reluctant elephant up a hill, it just doesn't seem to go where you would like it to. But, there is always more than one way to achieve a goal, and the Internet can expand these options even further.

Often we feel that we can only make money through our business if we are selling something to someone via our shop (whether online or in the high street). However, the Internet offers possibilities for more sophisticated ways of developing additional income streams that you may not have thought of before. This section of the book begins to take you on the journey to find complimentary products and services that you can add to your current business.

13. Passive vs active income

Active income is what we receive in return for doing something, for instance by going to work each week we are paid a salary, or we sell widgets on the Internet and each time we take an order, we process the payment, parcel it up, take it along to the Post Office and go home again.

Passive income on the other hand is what we earn when we aren't doing anything at all. We could be sunning ourselves in the Bahamas, be skiing in Gstaad or even having coffee with friends at the nice little deli that has just opened down the road - and we would still be earning income! A good example of passive income would be the interest you receive on your savings, you don't do anything as the interest just accrues as long as you leave the money in the account.

The Internet is full of ways to earn passive income and this book will give you many ideas for how you might be able to do it too. Of course, the most obvious ones are related to marketing other people's products and services, either directly or through affiliate links and pay-per-click schemes. But, if you really want to get into passive income, then you might want to take a look at creating your own digital products (documents, photo's, music, software) that can be delivered automatically to the customer - you simply have to monitor the process.

14. The ONLY 3 ways to build your business

Did you know there are only three ways you can build up your business? Yes, that's right, three ways whether it is online, offline, service or product based or any combination of those four. Ultimately, you have to either:

1. Increase the number of customers
2. Increase the price of your products
3. Increase the number of purchases each customer makes

Ideally you would like to do all three because that is where the greatest gains are going to be made. The secrets of how you might do some, or all of these, is contained within the rest of this book. Here are two questions for you to keep in mind when you are evaluating the various topics that this book covers....

• What is your turnover currently? _____

• What would it be if you were able to increase your business by each of the three ways listed above? _____

15. Calculate the value of your customers

Do you know what it costs you to get each one of your customers? Do you have any idea of how much you should be paying for advertising? If not, then you may be losing money.

It might be worth doing the following simple calculations which may help you think about what you might be able to do differently.

What we will calculate are:

- the sales conversion rate
- the sign-up conversion rate
- the sales per visitor rate

The Sales Conversion Rate (SCR): The sales conversion rate is the number of people that actually buy something from you and a good rate will be dependent on the market sector you are operating in. The calculation looks like this:

Number of Visitors to Your Site (shop or office) / Number of People That Bought

_____ ÷ _____ = _____

The Sign-up Conversion Rate (SCR): Your sign-up conversion rate is important because these people are potential customers and they are signing up to receive something from you (usually free of charge) such as a newsletter, literature or a free sample. When someone has signed up to receive whatever you are offering, you then have the opportunity to sell other products and services to them later on.

A site with good marketing should achieve a sign-up rate that is somewhere between 10% and 33% of visitors although this does depend on the site, what you are offering in return for their personal details and why your visitors might be looking for it. Here is the calculation:

Number of Visitors to Website (shop or office) / Number of People that Signed Up

_____ ÷ _____ = _____

Sales per Visitor (SPV) Rate: This will tell you how much each visitor is worth and therefore indicate how much you might spend on advertising in a pay per click promotion for instance. Take the amount of money you made in sales for any given period and then divide it by the number of visitors to your website, shop or office that you had for the same period (you should be able to find out your visitor statistics for your website from your web host). The calculation looks like this:

Visitor Numbers / Sales

_____ ÷ _____ = _____

Of course, there are many things that could affect all of these figures, such as seasonal fluctuations, holiday times, changes in policies at Government level etc... Overall however, they should provide you with a good way of monitoring how well your business is doing over the course of the next few months.

Why is it important to know all of these figures? Because as you systematically work out how to increase them, you will simultaneously increase your business income as well!

16. Keeping the customer happy

Imagine going into your local bookshop to find a book on preventing slug attacks in the garden. There is nothing on the shelves so you ask one of the assistants to check to see whether there is anything in the stock room. The assistant disappears; ten minutes later you are still waiting. So, you look for another assistant and relate your requirements all over again. This time the assistant looks it up on the computerised stock system and informs you that they don't have it but they can order it for you. You check that it will arrive in time to give to your mother-in-law at Christmas (it is early November after all), go ahead and place the order.

Two weeks later, you contact the shop to find out whether it has arrived, you are told that it hasn't yet, but they will let you know when it comes in. Another two weeks pass (it is now early December) and you still haven't heard anything, so you call again. "It hasn't arrived yet but I will ring the wholesaler and call you back in half an hour," you are told. Two days later you're still awaiting that return 'phone call and are beginning to get worried as the book is the only thing your mother-in-law has asked for. This time you go into the bookshop and speak to the manager who tells you that the book came in and was promptly sold to another customer, but they will order it again on 'special delivery'.......... and so it goes on, and on, and on ... until you give up and order from Amazon instead.

The purpose of this little tale is to let you know that the only thing that will ensure a successful business is fulfilling your customers expectations and even aiming to exceed them. There really is no point in having a fabulous looking place, on or off-line, with all the right products 'in stock' if your service isn't up to scratch or you cannot supply them.

It is worth bearing in mind that the Internet has had the effect of raising our expectations to expect instant gratification. If they order something today, they want to receive it within a couple of days (postal services permitting). What they don't expect is to wait 28 days for their order to be fulfilled. The web gives the impression of a 24/7 operation and if you intend to sell anything on the web then you need to take this into account.

As I write this, I am sitting in a hotel room in Malta. Although I have arranged for someone back home to ship orders, I am still needed to answer emails and deal with any problems that arise. My customers don't care whether I am in the office or not, they care about getting their orders on time and having their questions answered. I limit my time online keeping up with the really important questions that can't wait, the rest of the time I'm on the beach or visiting the sights.

I do all this because I never underestimate the importance of keeping my customers happy. It means they come back again in the future, they even recommend me to others that are interested in what I do, but above all, they seem to enjoy doing business with me.

17. Getting feedback

When you were employed, did you have regular feedback sessions with your line manager on your performance? It was probably called something like an Appraisal and may have covered whether you achieved your objectives, your attitude to work, what you could do to improve your performance as well as setting new goals for the coming months. This appraisal may even have a direct bearing on what you earned; if it was positive you were awarded a pay increment or a bonus and if it wasn't ... well you stayed on the same salary as last year, except that this year the cost of living was a bit higher so you felt a little worse off.

Whilst quality of life is often given as the main reason why people want to change their life/work balance, the second motivator may well be that it offers the opportunity to earn some serious money. But, and here's a thought for you, I think you still need to do that annual or six monthly appraisal of yourself because without it you may not learn where you could make a change or an improvement, you might not spot the latest trend and may even be losing sales. This time however, the person doing the appraisal is not your line manager, it should be your customers who, if you are very lucky, may be telling you what they like and dislike through the feedback you get. Feedback, even if it seems negative, is pure gold because it gives you an opportunity to improve things for both you and your customers.

If you are anything like me, then getting feedback can be a little daunting at first. It is like asking someone to tell you exactly what they think of you, warts and all. It opens your business up to all sorts of criticism that you may find hard to deal with initially. It is important to remember however, that your customers do not know YOU, they only know your service; it may feel a bit personal but it isn't - honestly. With feedback you get a frank appraisal of how well your business is doing. It will show you where you can improve and what you are doing really well. It may even show you how to tweak things to make them even better and best of all, it should give you many positive comments that you can then use in your marketing efforts.

However, people won't normally give you feedback unless it's to complain. To get other, more helpful forms of feedback you will need to ask for it. I send requests for feedback in emails sent out to customers after they have made a purchase or when their daily hints and tips have come to an end. This is extremely effective and means that I get several dozen emails every day, almost all overwhelmingly positive about the service I have provided. When you make a personal request to an individual in this way, it makes them feel valued, the fact that you have taken the time and trouble to ask that customer for their opinions matters to them. When I do get something negative or with a suggestion, I always try to look at it positively and see it from their perspective, and then I write and thank them for taking the time and trouble to get in touch. Just because I created the site or the product, doesn't mean to say it is 100% free of human error and everything can always be improved.

18. Acquiring stock

You have your business idea and you even have the business plan. Now all you have to do is source the goods you are planning to sell. In this respect, the web is no different from a high street shop. You need a supplier of goods to you, you will add a percentage on to the wholesale price and, after fixed costs, and this will be your profit. Unless you are only selling one or two things that come your way each month on Ebay, you are going to have to find someone to supply you with your products.

However, you may be selling your own craft products or the book you have written, in which case this hint may not be too relevant unless you want to diversify into related products. This is a strategy I have used to great effect with The Hysterectomy Association; initially we only sold our own books, but then I added a couple of relevant books that I source from book wholesalers, later I included products for post-operative support.

You could try finding a wholesaler by asking your competitors who they use, you would be surprised at how accommodating they can be.

You might decide to sell second hand books or clothes; in which case regular visits to local charity shops could be all you need to do; car boot, yard sales and small ads in local newspapers may also do the trick.

You may even find stock online especially on Ebay, try the wholesale section for ideas. Finally, local shops may provide you with stock at reduced cost if you buy in bulk, it may even be possible to collaborate with one that doesn't already have an online presence.

The short guide to websites

Jimmy insisted on sampling all the tortilla chips he was
planning to sell on his new website!
© Photographer: Pusicmario | Agency: Dreamstime.com

Websites are funny creatures: one minute they are there, the next they can vanish in a puff of smoke. Some people might tell you that if you want to do business using the Internet, the only thing you can do is have a website; well I'm here to tell you otherwise. A business is a little like a birthday cake, it has many slices to it and your website - should you chose to have one - is only ever going to be a single slice. The moral of this is, don't let it become an all-consuming behemoth that takes all your time and energy as it is possible to have a very successful online business without a website at all!

19. Do you really need a website?

Why do you want a website? I think I can guarantee that it is almost certainly one of the following reasons:-

1. Everybody else has one
2. A business advisor told me I needed one
3. My friend (daughter, husband, mother, son) said they would do it free
4. It seemed like a good idea at the time

So, I'll ask the question again, do you really need a website? This question isn't as strange as it sounds in a book about online business. There are many ways you can use the Internet for your business without ever having to worry about a domain name, web address, or website, although this will depend on what you are doing to some extent.

For instance, you could sell exclusively on Ebay with, or without, one of their shops. You might use Amazon market place and ABE Books to sell second-hand books (or even new ones for that matter). You may decide that you are simply going into affiliate marketing with a Google Adwords account. I think what I am trying to encourage you not to do, is to develop a website simply because you think you should; they take money to get right, time to develop and mature, and can be problematic when they go wrong - so only do it if it really will help your business be more effective.

20. The single page or sales letter

The simplest website, if you do decide you need one, is a 'single page'. This is often a sales letter exhorting a visitor to part with their hard-earned cash. Beloved of web marketeers, there are many different styles of single page. You can view examples at **growabetterbusiness.co.uk** to give you some ideas.

However, their biggest drawback is that they are just too darned long and their call to action often happens at the end. If you have ever printed one out, you may have found that they can be anything from five to twenty pages. Although, they are intended to be read on your computer screen, reading a web page on a computer screen is very hard on the eyes and most people prefer not do it for too long.

In addition to their length, they can be notoriously difficult to get a decent ranking on the natural search results of the main search engines simply because they have no real content, other than a 'sales pitch'. If a visitor doesn't like what they see, they usually return to the list of search results very quickly, indicating that the site wasn't what they were looking for. If there is one thing that search engines dislike about a website it is when the use of the back button indicates that the information was not relevant and relevancy, for Google and it's cohorts, is the key attribute when it comes to search engine ranking.

21. The domain name low down

In order to set up your own business website, you will need a web address, an account with a website hosting company (some of the better ones have been listed on the website at **growabetterbusiness.co.uk**), some files or software loaded onto your patch of online real estate and the information you would like to include.

When you purchase a domain name think about who your customers will be. If they are based mainly in the UK then choose a domain name that ends in '.uk', choosing a .com address can result in alienating your customers as the address suggests that you are based in the US.

A web address is as personal as your home address or your telephone number. It can only ever point to a single web site, just as your phone number is related to your home address. Having your own web address means that you are not restricted in any way by a hosting company and you are free (within the bounds of the law of course) to do what you want with the address that you have. If you have the right address, it can, in its own way, create a brand or an image that people come to recognise (you only have to think of Google, ebay, or Amazon to recognise this). You can put it on your business stationery; you can add it to your listing in the yellow pages or advertise it in the tabloid press. You can do all of these things without worrying that it might disappear or be removed, just as long as you keep paying the bi-annual fees.

It is also worth remembering that you don't have to host your site with the same company that you bought your web address from. You can buy your web address from one company and host the site with another; you will simply need to *'point'* your web address to the hosting you have purchased. This means that you can pay as little as possible for the web address and then find the best value host as well, and I can assure you that the two do not necessarily go together.

In addition, and with a little setting up, your web address can also be used in your email address. So instead of having janey326@hotmail.com you can become jane@mysite.co.uk instead, which looks far more professional.

22. Free or fee?

It is easily possible to get a website completely free of charge; you may have been given some webspace by your internet service provider, or you could sign up for a free 'blog. However, free is not necessarily the benefit it might seem. Using a free service may mean that you need to put up with advertising that you have no control over, it may limit the number of people who can visit you, it could restrict what you can do and could prevent you from selling items through it and it could even drop off this virtual 'mortal coil'. Although, if you are simply presenting an online brochure about your services then it may be a useful way of dipping your toe in the water so to speak; and if it proved successful, you could graduate to something more professional later on.

However, this is where the single page might just benefit you. Often when you buy a domain name (and remember you can get them for very little money), you may be given the opportunity to create a very simple website, often just one or two pages, completely free of charge. This would be more than enough for some information about your product, your contact details and a 'buy now' button from PayPal. They can work and I have used this technique several times before. I use one company for almost all of my domain names and webhosting, and they provide a free page service. It is very easy to use: simply choose a template, type the information you want to include and away you go.

23. Free software

When the web first began, each page had to be carefully crafted using something called 'hypertext mark-up language'. This wasn't too difficult for those that were familiar with the pre-windows versions of MS Word, but it wasn't easy to generate something that looked smart either, in fact, it was de-rigour to use as many different colours, fonts and flashing text as possible. As a result, my first web sites were very dodgy looking to say the least!

Nowadays however, there is a lot of free software around that you can use if you feel brave enough to download it and you will find some of it listed and linked to on my website at *growabetterbusiness.co.uk*. In fact, some of this software may even come pre-loaded within the hosting packages offered by a few of the more enlightened hosting companies.

The only downside to using free software is that you may have to install it yourself which may take a bit of time and knowledge, and you may feel it is too difficult or time consuming. If this is the case, then setting up a domain name and purchasing a hosting account with one of the larger hosting companies around might be more appropriate. This is because they have many tools built into their accounts that you can simply 'turn on' when you want to use them. They also have excellent sets of tutorials and a help desk that you can call if you get stuck.

24. Content management software

Back in the old days, a web developer would create an initial page, let's call it the home page: this would usually have some writing about the company on it and a picture. In order to create this one page the developer had to create two files on the computer, the first was a text file that contained all the words a visitor would read as well as all the '*coding*', which instructed a visitors computer how the page should be displayed. The second file was the picture file. Every time a new page was added to the site, the same process had to be followed. Each page was created manually and was linked to the previous pages via some sort of list containing links that visitors could click on.

However, as websites developed and became larger it was more difficult to keep creating pages in this very laborious way - just imagine doing that for all the books on Amazon. This led to the development of content management software (CMS) which allowed website developers to use a database to store information separately from the design of the site. Life suddenly became much easier because all the website owner had to do was concentrate on what they wanted to say. All of my websites now use some sort of CMS to manage them, although they aren't all using the same one.

If you are thinking about setting up a website then I would strongly recommend getting hold of some content management software. Fortunately some of the best come free of charge, although you may have to install it yourself. I use Wordpress for most of my sites because it is so easy and I use Joomla and PHPBB for another. Once installed they are reasonably simple to use - you simply login in and create a new page or item of information and then update the menu's if necessary. Links to the latest information can be shown automatically on the home page so that visitors can see what is new immediately (this is great for search engine ranking as well) and it's a doddle to find your way around as well. You can even try out Wordpress free of charge and set up an account very quickly by visiting ***www.wordpress.com***.

25. Lies, damn lies and statistics

I know that there is an underlying belief that you can make statistics say anything you want, but please don't dismiss them in the context of the web. These sorts of statistics are incredibly useful because they can help you find out which pages are the most popular and which country your visitors are based in as well as a host of other interesting and useful facts.

The statistics will tell you which web browser people are using and when your site is most active. They may be able to show you trends across the year - for instance, I know that fewer people come to The Hysterectomy Association website during the summer months and at holiday times.   Having said all that, they won't be able to tell you why these trends occur and you may need to make a few assumptions along the way.

Statistics may also be able to tell you how people found you, and which search terms they used in a search engine or whether they typed your address in directly to their browser. They will be able to give you some idea of how many return visitors you get (simply by dividing the total number of visitors by the number of unique visitors) or how 'sticky' your site is (by dividing the number of page views by the number of visitors). Even though this isn't an exact science it will provide you with very useful guidance.

What the statistics cannot tell you though is the name of the person visiting you nor their address, bank account details or any other personal information.   Therefore, the information gleaned from the statistics is great for tweaking your site and working out what to do more, or less of (by using the pages that are most and least visited). But they aren't good for working out who exactly your visitors are; to do that you would need to use more sophisticated market research methods that are outside of the scope of this hint, or even this book.

Most hosting packages these days include this statistical information as a matter of course. If they do not appear to be available in your account, call the help desk and ask how to get access to them. The hosting company's servers will be recording the information anyway, so giving you access to the file shouldn't be a problem.

26. Keep it simple

The web can be a complicated and fearful place for many people. Just think back to when you were first introduced to the Internet, how did you find out how to use it? Was it trial and error or did you have to ask for help?

I bet it was a mixture of the two; even now I come across things I have never seen before and I first used the Internet in the mid 1980's - long before the web was born. Make your online offerings as simple as possible so that everyone understands what you want them to do. This is as important for an advertising campaign as it is for a website or a music download. Don't make your message clever or so obscure that it will only appeal to those with the time, and inclination, to work out what you are trying to say; unless it is a service for readers of the New Oxford Dictionary of course!

If you are selling spades, tell people you are selling spades, do not tell them you are selling digging implements as that may be confusing and they might go somewhere else instead. Make it obvious that they buy spades by clicking on the link marked 'spades'. Using a combination of words and pictures may be helpful, especially if you have customers that don't speak the same language. One word of advice though, avoid using only pictures because images mean different things to different people.

You also need to be aware of local subtleties. For instance, a hot *flush* to a woman in the UK is a hot *flash* to a woman in the US, and conversely a hot flash to someone from the UK has yet another highly inappropriate meaning! I have also lost count of the number of times I've had to email someone back to say that my spelling is not wrong and that the Hysterectomy Association website is based in the UK where the spelling is different. You may have noticed some apparent misspellings in this book or on the website as well for the same reason. Finally, try to steer clear of jargon though, unless you have a seriously restricted market place where everyone uses the same language and terminology.

27. Don't play about with design

Most users of the web are used to links on the left or right hand side of the page as well as across the top; they do not like frames; they do not like scrolling down a page (although this could depend on what they are looking at). And they definitely don't like scrolling across a page horizontally so do make sure your web design fits into any size of screen (within reason). Don't use flash movies as entry pages as it wastes a click; people expect to click on a link in Google, go straight to a website and see what they need to do immediately.

Make it obvious what actions you would like them to take when they get to your website; whether it is to get information, sign up for tips, download a document or buy something. If they are going to buy something, let them buy it with as little fuss as possible, don't make them go through endless pages asking for more and more personal information - limit it to what they want, the number they want, how they want it shipped, their contact details and their payment information. You do not need to know their shoe size, the name of their dog, where they were born and what they had for breakfast this morning (unless you are a cobbler, dog walker, astrologer or cereal producer!).

More importantly, don't limit who can look at your website by telling them *"this site is best viewed in Internet Explorer 5.9.8.7.5.0.4 at 800 x 600"*. All this does is annoy people like me who use another browser and who resent the fact that you want me to change my browsing habits just to make your design work. I'll go elsewhere for my Jimmy Choo's thank you very much! Incidentally, using some form of content management system will eliminate most of these problems as they are designed to work across all browsers.

If you want to know what makes a good, easy to use website visit Jakob Neilsen's website, *useit.com* - where you can follow the debate about what defines good (and bad) web design.

28. Blogging

Blogging (short for web log - an online diary of sorts) is one of the new kids on the Internet block and you may well have bought a copy of this book from one of my 'blogs. But I wouldn't want to imply that 'blogging has only just begun, it hasn't. I first became aware of it in 1999 and there are now estimated to be well over two million of them (and counting, by the time you read this the number will have grown considerably - you can check out *www.blogcensus.net* for the latest estimates.) However, not all blogs are maintained, some are ephemeral things that appear one day and are dead, or dying, the next. I should know, I've started a few of those as well.

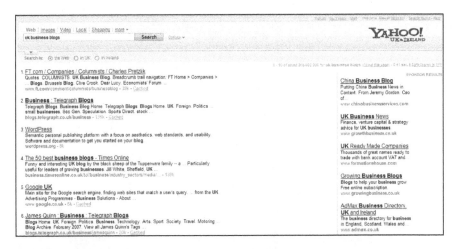

But how can it help in your quest to make millions by lunchtime tomorrow? Well, it can be one of the easiest ways to start a website, taking as little as a few minutes if you use an instant service. There is no configuring to do, no code to write and you don't have to host it yourself either if you don't want to (although this can be beneficial for marketing reasons). They are regularly indexed by search engines (so helping you to get visitors to your site) and you can sell from them. With pages about a product and a PayPal link, you can be earning money from day one; you can even run syndicated adverts in some 'blogging software. However, not all blogs are created equal and you will need to do a little research before you get started.

You do need a topic or theme around which your 'blog revolves; this could be how to dye your hamster day-glo pink, employment law or your new service for vacuum cleaners.

I mentioned earlier that it would be helpful to have your blog hosted on your own domain. This is because you have more control over how it operates and you won't lose anything valuable in the way of information, data or your search engine ranking if something happens to, or changes at, the free hosting company. However, if you want to take the, albeit minimal, risk that it might all crash down around your ears, go for a free blog that is hosted for you - it is infinitely easier after all.

There are a huge number of alternatives when it comes to blog hosting and software. Personally, I prefer WordPress because you can also download the software for your own website, as well as host one free of charge at **wordpress.com**.

Unfortunately, the hosted version won't allow you to use the many add-ons that are available and this means that earning an income from syndicated adverts won't be available to you, but if you download the software and run it on your own domain name then you have complete control over all these aspects.

Blogger is another very popular 'blogging tool which is also owned by Google, which may mean that it is indexed more easily. It will also allow you to use a Google Adsense account and so earn money from advertising. However, if you do decide at some point to upgrade from a free version, then you won't be able to do this with Blogger unless you re-create the whole site from scratch. This is because the Blogger software isn't available to download and you can't pick up the database either. Interestingly however, you can 'pull' the information from a blogger site into a Wordpress site if you wanted to!

29. Landing pages

A landing page is, obviously, the place at which someone lands on your website whenever they follow a link. Yes, I know, I may be teaching my mother to suck eggs here; but there are landing pages, and there are landing pages and they are not all made equal.

The home page of a website is a landing page; it may also be the page that is linked to from a search engine's natural search results. Therefore, it needs to have very clear information saying what the site is about with lots of easy to spot links to the rest of the information. If you are advertising on the Internet, then you will probably want to create a specific landing page for each and every advert. Landing pages have to be as easy to use as the home page, so that the visitor is able to see immediately what you expect them to do; whether that is buy something, sign up for something, telephone someone or go somewhere else. But what happens if someone doesn't want to do what you would like them to do?

This is one of the great debates of the Internet marketing world - should a landing page be a single web page, with no links to anywhere else; or should it be part of a bigger website. Both have their advantages and disadvantages and what you choose to do may well depend on what you are 'selling'.

If your landing page is a single page, then you run the risk of people hitting the back button to return to the search engine listings. This action has the effect of telling the search engine that your site isn't compelling enough and therefore not as relevant as others for that particular search term, which will naturally impact on your placement in their listings.

However, if your landing page is part of a larger website, then people might get to it and find themselves a little like a child in a sweet shop - they want to explore everything NOW and as a result lose the impetus to do whatever it is you wanted them to do. The advantage of this one though is that the search engines will love you because your site is interesting and absorbing to your visitors.

Finally, you could even do what I once did with a landing page on The Hysterectomy Association website, and add lots of links to other people's website's - now that really was stupid! Why was it stupid? Because I had just paid to have quality visitors directed to my website and here I was promoting someone else instead.

30. Quality vs quantity

Don't necessarily assume that having one million visitors to your website every day is going to be a good thing. Firstly, if you have this many visitors it is likely that your hosting company will be charging you extra for the additional load that your site is putting on their services. Secondly the servers and databases you are using may not be able to handle that number of simultaneous visitors either and could result in your website being unavailable to potential customers.

However, if you have an information only website then you may be chasing visitor numbers just to increase the revenue you might get from companies advertising on your site. On the other hand, if you are planning to sell a product or service then you want to attract only those who are actively looking for what you are offering.

To increase the quality of visitors to your website, i.e. those who are specifically interested in the product or service you are offering, you need to be very clear about what you want your intended audience to do by making this obvious on each page with the use of page titles, headings and text. This also has the effect of helping the search engines index you correctly and will increase the relevancy of your information. When you decide to run a pay-per-click campaign yourself, do make sure that the words in your ad match the content of the pages you are sending people to as it helps make sure that your advert is shown to the greatest number of Google searchers. Remember, having one customer that buys something is better than ten visitors who are just looking!

31. The joy of email

Email is one of those tools that seems to have become endemic in the Western world and, a little like texting, it has a language and formality (or informality) all of it's own. However, there are a few unwritten rules that you would do well to remember. The most important of these is to be aware that whatever you say in an email can form a 'contract' in the same way as a written set of terms and conditions do. Therefore, if you can't deliver a widget by next Tuesday, don't say you can.

Do you have any bad habits when it comes to email? For instance, I was one of those people who constantly checked to see if any email had arrived and I often found I had done little else all day other than deal with email. Eventually I changed the way I worked; I now deal with all my email first thing in the morning. Everything is dealt with once a day; as a result I am less stressed, I feel more productive and I finally have time to do the other things in my life.

You also need to consider the concept of 'good' and 'bad' email techniques. I've summarised the most important points to bear in mind below:-

1. Write an appropriate subject line - this helps your recipient decide whether to open the email or not. Bear in mind that if you regularly send emails with an inappropriate subject line, you will find the people start to delete them without even thinking about opening them.
2. Don't reply to the group - reply to the sender instead. There is nothing worse than receiving a dozen emails from people

all saying that 'yes they can attend the meeting at 10.00 tomorrow'.

3. If you are sending an email out to a large group of people keep their address private by using the BCC (blind carbon copy) facility.

4. Keep it brief - your recipient will make a decision about whether they have the time to read your latest novel or bin it.

5. Give me a context as I probably don't know you from Adam or can't remember your name from the networking event we were at last week.

6. Ensure you give your recipient a clear idea of what it is you expect them to do next.

7. If there is a deadline, say there is a deadline.

8. Don't keep asking if they have received your email; once is OK, any more is rude.

32. Don't ignore your customers

If you are planning to use the Internet in your business, it is important that you remember to check your email - I have lost count of the number of companies I come across that never reply to my enquiries. Please, please, don't ignore your email; a customer may be having difficulty downloading your document or signing up for your newsletter; they may be complimenting you on your exemplary website or they may want your postal address to send a nice fat cheque. Why not use yourself as a guide? When you send an email to someone how long do you wait for a reply before you start to get impatient? Five minutes, 24 hours or a week? Whatever the figure is, you need to apply that to your customers and maybe reduce it by half. I can't stress strongly enough, the web is a 24/7 environment and people using it don't factor in that you have to sleep, need to eat or take a holiday occasionally.

If you are likely to get lots of email then it might be wise to invest in an autoresponse message that says an email has been received and will be getting your attention very soon and that they can expect a reply within ..., well you set the time frame as you know your business. BUT, when you do give a time frame make sure you follow through on it - people don't want to be told to expect a reply within 48 hours and then wait a week; if they had been a potential customer this could be what turns them into the non-purchaser. Remember the business maxim *'under promise and over deliver'*.

I also have a policy of replying to people who are telling me how much they like (or dislike) the book, the tips, or the website. This is because I'm grateful that they have taken some of their valuable time to give me feedback that will help improve my products and services. I try to make each reply to these emails as personal as possible - including a detail they have written such as important dates or names so that they can see a real person has read it and is responding. Email is the main communication tool of the Internet so it pays to use it well.

Preparing for Legal Eagles and the Taxman

Giles hoped the judge would let him off with a warning!
© Photographer: Pusicmario | Agency: Dreamstime.com

Okay, so you have a product or service to sell, you have the office and a website - is there anything else you need to do? Well yes there is (and this is the boring bit), but it is the bit that could just save you a whole load of money if you do it now, and do it right. This is the legal and business critical 'stuff' that could land you before a judge just like Giles if you don't take it on board. I can assure you that lack of knowledge is no defence in court. Just because you might only be working on the Internet does not exempt you either, you are still bound by the laws of the country in which you work and in some cases the laws of the countries you supply to as well.

This whole section will cover the main elements you need to consider when complying with legal requirements and tax issues, and could be the best bit of bedtime reading you do!

33. Contact details

Every business website must display contact details, including a real world address, for the business owner/company. It is a legal responsibility in Europe and the US that you provide a way for people to contact you if they have any sort of problem with your product or service.

However, this is actually a plus point because would you buy from someone who only gave their hotmail email address? But if they tell you that their business address is 59 Something Street, Somewhere, Place, County, TTG 9JU, UK - would that make you feel more comfortable? Whilst these details aren't a cast iron guarantee that the company you are dealing with is kosher, you can at least check that they exist. So, if that makes you feel more confident, imagine what it will do for your customers!

34. Telephone numbers

You should provide a telephone number as well and I would recommend that this is not a cell 'phone or mobile number; but an actual landline number that customers can call you on. Not only will you comply with the law, but also it will give your customers a nice warm feeling that they can actually talk with you or your staff if they want to. A telephone number can also be a selling feature, especially if you say people can contact you when they have a question. Although you might worry that you will end up receiving 100's of calls a day, the reality is that you will probably only get one or two a week.

I'd also like to give you a further incentive to add a telephone number to your contact details as, with the right sort of number, you can be paid every time someone calls you. And how is this done? By using premium or national rate phone numbers (900 and 800 phone numbers in the US).

I have a telephone help line that clients can call for information and support as well as to order the products I sell over the telephone. Each time someone rings, I earn a proportion of the call revenue. Even better, I can move offices from one part of the country to another - and the number goes with me.

These telephone lines can be used for anything from an information service, to taking telephone orders or even as your private telephone number if you move around the country a lot. The amount of revenue can vary hugely and some providers will charge a set-up fee whilst others won't, so you do need to check the small print before signing up. There is a list of providers for the UK and the US on the resources pages of the website so do check them out and make it worth your while answering the telephone!

35. Legal issues to be considered

If you are trading online, you are legally required to provide the following pieces of information for your customers:-

- Terms and Conditions of Service that cover how you run your business. They must include information on how you will handle returns, how you deal with shipping and how much it costs if that isn't detailed in the checkout process, what the complaints procedure is and how you attempt to resolve problems. You might also include what is and isn't acceptable use of your website especially if you allow your customers to post up their own comments!

- A Disclaimer, especially if you are offering information that people might use to determine a particular course of action - for instance health, financial or legal information.

- You also have to include information about your qualifications and the professional bodies that you are a member of, if it pertains to your business.

I would strongly suggest that you have someone who is legally qualified look over any documents you create before you release them on an unsuspecting public, as you never know when you just might trip yourself up otherwise.

36. Privacy & The Data Protection Act

According to the office of the Information Commissioner, *"All public and private organisations are legally obliged to protect any personal information they hold."* Every business in the UK that collects personal data is required to register as a Data Controller and declare the uses that they have for the information they gather. If you think this doesn't apply to you, you need to think again. Every business collects personal information; you need it to be able to process orders for instance, you may have employees or enquirers, or you may be sending out a regular newsletter.

In the majority of circumstances, you will need to register with the Information Commissioner. It will cost £35 to complete the registration and needs to be updated each year. You can apply online through the website at: ***www.ico.gov.uk***

You should also let your visitors and customers know what you do with the information they give you in the form of a privacy statement. This tells them what you do to protect their personal information and whether you share it with anyone else, such as a marketing company or your accountant for instance. You might want to link this in to your Data Protection registration if you are based in the UK.

37. Copyright

Copyright is automatically assigned whenever you create something unique, whether it is a book, a website, your latest 'blog article or a song. You cannot copy anybody else's work unless you ask them if you can. Which means you should not go around using the copy and paste function to add content to your website. There is sophisticated software that will search for any copyrighted content and the financial penalties, if caught, can be severe - you have been warned!

You might also want to add watermarks to any images you create which will discourage people from using them without your permission. Finally, whilst it isn't a requirement, I would recommend that you include a copyright statement on anything you produce, whether it is a document or a web page. It is normally displayed like this one: © 2008, Linda Parkinson-Hardman

38. Accessibility

All website's have a legal responsibility to make their sites accessible to the disabled. This might mean ensuring that voice readers for the blind will work with the site, or that you have a nice easy to 'read' text version. It may be that some of your information needs to be made available in braille or as an MP3 so that people can listen instead of read. Once again, lack of knowledge is no defence and to make sure that your website complies you should get it checked out to see if it is 'bobby' compatible (*www.accessible.org/bobby-approved.html*). The WW3C (world wide web consortium) has lots of information on current web standards as well and will give you hints and tips about how to improve your website.

39. Cookies

A Cookie is a small piece of information that is downloaded to your home or office PC when you visit a website. It might be used to store your username and password for a website, or they may track what you do when you use a website - these sorts of cookies are what power the web statistics we talked about earlier.

However, they will not gather personal information about you, or your visitors, unless you specifically tell them that information in the first place, such as when you place an order for something. A good example would be giving your name and email address to **growabetterbusiness.co.uk** to receive the five day e-course or my weekly hints and tips. I don't know anything else about you, just your first name and email address, and you can remove yourself from that list at any time.

The only time that cookies might be a bit risky is if you are using publicly accessible computers, such as those in Internet cafes, to work on things like your email accounts. If you do find yourself doing this whilst on holiday for instance, I would recommend that each time you finish you clear the history, cookies and any downloaded files on the computer. This is simply a precaution that will prevent the casual observer from making assumptions about what you have been doing. Of course, it goes without saying that you **NEVER** click on **YES** when you get that little pop-up box that asks if you want to store your password on any public computer - what you get up to in the privacy of your own home is however between you and your laptop!

40. Taxing the business

According to Benjamin Franklin, there are only two certainties in life; death and taxes. And yes, if you are doing anything more than selling your unwanted items on Ebay you will be accruing additional income and this may well mean that you need to pay additional taxes. What additional taxes you will need to pay and how you would declare them will depend on the country you are resident in.

You may also need to be aware of double taxation issues (that is being taxed in your own Country AND by another Government). This is especially true if you are earning royalties in the US and are not a US Citizen.

When you sign up for some US owned online services such as Google Adsense or Ebay you may well be required to download a tax form W-8BEN to complete and return before you are able to open an account. In some cases, you may even need a US Taxpayer Identification Number, even though you aren't a US citizen, if you want to avoid double taxation.

One of my strongest recommendations would be to keep accurate records. Not only will these be useful for completing your tax return, you will also be able to present them as evidence if there is ever any query. In the UK, we need to keep accounting records for seven years although this may be different in other countries.

As a minimum you will need to keep income and expenditure information and don't forget that if you also employ staff then you will have another whole taxation issue to deal with as well.

There may also be state taxes to account for if you are based in the US and finally you may need to register for VAT (value added tax) in the UK and Europe if you start to make over the current lower limit for registration (£64,000 per annum and £16,000 per quarter in February 2008 in the UK, although it may be different in other countries). For more information on the taxes that may apply in your case visit the website where you will find a whole range of links to different organisations and articles that might be helpful.

41. Insurance

Do you need insurance for your business? This is not a trick question I can assure you, and it may be wise to consider it. Here are just a few of the areas that might be relevant:-

- Does your household insurance allow you to run a business from home? (household contents and buildings insurance)
- Does your car insurance cover business use, as well as running to and from your place of work? (car insurance)
- Will you employ anybody to help you run your online business? (employers liability insurance)
- Might customers come to your home to collect or purchase items? (public liability insurance)
- Will you be selling and shipping high value items that might get lost en-route to their destination? (you might use the insurance provided by your shipper)
- Will you have valuable stock stored in your garage or attic? (business/stock insurance)
- Are you giving advice to people? (professional indemnity policies that protect you in the event of a claim)

The website has links to all sorts of sites and other information that may help you to determine if you have any insurance issues that need to be considered.

Introducing Marketing In The Online World

Henry couldn't understand why no one was going to his website!

© Photographer: Dejan Savic | Agency: Dreamstime.com

The success of any venture lies in the way that the product (or service) is marketed. As my darling husband has said to me often enough "*some of the best ideas in the world are simply filling stock room shelves*" and why? Because they never sold, that's why. I know I run the risk of being accused of stating the obvious, but you do need to sell your product (or service) if you want to be successful, and to increase the likelihood of making big bucks then you need to sell either one very, very expensive item once a year, or several hundred less expensive items every month. Whichever way you choose to go, you are going to have to sell your product (or service) to the people that are most likely to buy it. And how are these people going to find out about this amazing product (or service) that you have to offer? They are going to find out about it through the marketing (and advertising) that you do.

42. Marketing or advertising

What is the difference between marketing and advertising? Put simply, advertising is the poster campaign you run, it is the banner ad you create to put on some else's website, it is a TV commercial or the small ad in the newspaper. It is all about getting a message across to your audience very simply, quickly and easily about what your product or service is and how people can buy it.

Marketing on the other hand is a completely different ball game and is all about creating a recognisable brand. Sure, it includes the advertising campaign, but it also includes the message that you are hoping to get across on your website. It is the colour scheme you choose for your headed paper, the logo you have designed or the packaging that you use to ship your goods to their new owners. It is also about identifying who you want to sell your product to and then making sure that the 'look and feel' appeals to that target market.

Marketing is the image that you project with every aspect of your business - it tells people (sometimes subconsciously) that you are a good person to do business with, that you always follow through on your promises and that you are a professional in every sense of that word. Marketing, just like the advertising campaign, has to be planned; and it is probably better if you plan the overall image you want to project before you even contemplate the advertising aspect, because otherwise that could just be money wasted.

43. Market research

To begin the marketing process you need to have a clear idea of who your target audience are? Can you say you know who they are? Don't just say everyone, because not everyone is going to want to buy your product or service. Some people will be more inclined than others to take up your offer and who these people are may be based on their current situation, whether they have cash to spend, what social strata they occupy etc... I mean can you imagine the Queen in a Kiss Me Quick hat from Blackpool? No, neither can I.

Here is a little exercise to do before you start anything else at all. Write down a brief description of your product (or service). Try to do it in two paragraphs or less. Then write a list of all the reasons someone might buy it. Once you have your list, have a good look at what you have written; have you been entirely honest with yourself or is there anything else you can add to the list?   Now ask your friends and family what words they might use to try to define or find the product or service and then why they might pick your version over someone else's?

Now that you have this list I'd like you to write down what people need to have in order to buy your product (or service). This could be anything from a garden to a computer, significant amounts of money or even a sore throat. What I am hoping is that as you write these lists you begin to identify the groups of people that you might be able to target your product or service towards. You may also spot trends that mean it is better sell in the summer rather than the winter (or vice versa), that it is a one-off purchase that doesn't need to be repeated (like this book) or something that is ongoing, such as gym membership. Perhaps it is a 'casual buy' like the sweets at the checkout in the supermarket. Once you have identified all these possibilities you will then be able to get on with your marketing and advertising.

The next step is to find out what is really happening on the ground. Talk to people about your product or service, show them samples or ask if they might buy it. You could have a look at ebay to find out what people are actually paying or check out the high street and yellow pages. Research like this is invaluable and could save you the heartache of creating something that people don't actually want or need.

44. Free

Don't underestimate the power of the word **FREE**. Most people, if they are honest, are attracted to something they think is **FREE** even though they know that there is no such thing as a free lunch. Use the word Free in your advertising and you will attract visitors to whatever it is you are offering. However, if you want to use this form of marketing then you do need to be prepared to accept that the majority of visitors will never go beyond the free items. But once you can accept these two basic facts, then it becomes a powerful tool in your attempt to take over the world with your latest gerbil 'blog.

But how can you use it to your benefit and still make a decent living? Perhaps the most effective way is to give something that is of value in itself, but which may create an additional need that you can then fulfil through the products or services you are selling. Look at accountants, lawyers, counsellors or life coaches who usually give their potential clients an initial session free of charge so that both parties can assess whether the 'business' relationship is going to be successful or not. Take note of the wine merchants or supermarkets that regularly do free tastings of nibbly bits or drinks in order to develop a market. And what about 'buy two get one free offers, which encourage the customer already wanting to purchase a book, to buy extra simply because they will get something 'free of charge'.

Only you can really decide how you might apply the word **FREE** in your business because it is only you that knows what your business idea is. Over the years I have used the following techniques with varying degrees of success:-

- I have created free online communities to encourage people to return to the websites frequently
- Free hints and tips that are delivered by email (you may have decided to buy this book as a result of an email series),
- I have written additional free booklets or reports that people can download.
- I have found other reports and offers that my customers and users might find helpful and/or supportive
- I have added lots of free information

But it is always a fine line to tread; between giving too much away so that your users feel so saturated they don't need what you are trying to sell, and not giving enough so that they go elsewhere instead. And do remember that whatever it is you are doing on the Internet, ultimately it is all about information and the information you are selling is probably available somewhere free of charge as long as users have the patience to try and track it down.

Ultimately, the purpose of 'free', is to connect with your customers so that a bond of trust develops between you which can transcend the impersonal nature of the Internet and make them feel that they are valued.

45. Offline advertising

Don't dismiss the need for offline advertising and marketing even for a business that may exist solely on the Internet, as these can generate significant amounts of direct traffic to a website. I'll bet you didn't come across Ebay by doing a search on Yahoo. And I'm sure you didn't find the book you wanted through Google. You probably went straight to an online bookstore didn't you? Sites such as Amazon and Ebay have very strong offline brands that are instantly recognisable to much of the Western world. They have also used TV, radio and poster campaigns to increase awareness of their services. It would be fair to say that the dot.com boom and bust was created because businesses assumed that they no longer had to think about the real world.

You also need to think about what you can do offline, because relying solely on the search engines or online advertising can be very limiting. For instance, The Hysterectomy Association is listed in many different publications, such as help directories, on literature provided by the big health insurance companies like BUPA, we are recommended by many GP's, hospitals, gynaecologists and NHS Direct lists us on its telephone help line. We are listed in the resource sections of books and hospital leaflets and the last page of one of our downloaded booklets has an A4 sized poster that we ask the reader to print out for their local hospital or Doctors surgery. We also work with universities, researchers, journalists and the media, providing research materials, case studies as well as support for story lines and articles.

We do all of these things, because not everyone that might use our services is going to find us on the Internet; not everyone that needs us is going to have a computer at home or at work - and the same may be true of your customers. Incidentally, this is why we also let people order our books by telephone with their credit card or by order form and cheque.

Don't limit your customers by only using the Internet to advertise. Depending on what you are doing, you could put small ads in local newspapers, posters in shops or other places where people congregate, you might do an article or advertorial (mix of advert and editorial) to submit to the national media, you could have a telephone help line or even a brochure to send out full of additional information and an order form. The easiest way to find out what might work would be to look at your competitors and see what they are doing. Aim to be the only supplier in your chosen market place that regularly exceeds customers' expectations and then shout it from the rooftops.

46. Yell.com

Yell.com is the online version of the yellow pages in the UK. It lists all sorts of businesses around Great Britain, just like the physical yellow pages you may have in your home. If you run any sort of business you can get a basic entry free of charge that will include your business name, address and contact telephone number. If you have a website you can add a link to it for a small fee. Of course, you may not be a UK based business and I appreciate that you may not want, nor be able to advertise with Yell, so why not visit *www.ability.org.uk/phone.html* which gives a complete list of yellow pages around the world.

Of course there are other online and printed directories as well, that may be specific to a local area or to a particular type of business. Seek them out and see if you can add your business details to their listings - you never know just where the right sort of customer might come from.

47. Natural search ranking

One of the first search engines ever to appear was AltaVista. For a long time it had the biggest database of them all, in fact it probably does still have one of the largest databases. Then came Yahoo! and a whole host of others, until finally Google appeared on the scene. Search engines are being created, refined and developed all the time so who knows what we will see in the future. The one thing that characterises all of them though is that they provide a service that gives a user a list of links to follow when they search for something specific. These lists are often called natural search listings and they are lists of sites that the search engine has determined are the closest results it could find in its' database to the search term that you used. You will often find that search engines also offer a number of highlighted results as well; either at the top or in a different column and these are paid for advertisements which also match the search terms used.

Getting a high ranking in the natural search listings is key to attracting a lot of traffic to your website and you will need to do some work on your site to have it compete with 100's, 1000's or even 10,000's that compete with you for those visitors. In many ways this is easy because you simply need lots of very good and **relevant** information, yet it can be difficult to achieve consistency across all search services because the different search engines use different algorithms (mathematical equations) to determine which of the many sites they have listed are the most relevant to particular search requests.

If you do a search for 'hysterectomy' on **google.co.uk** you will probably find that we come out at number one or two in the natural search listings; if you do the same search on **google.com** then we may be listed somewhere on the first page. If you do the same search on **yahoo.com** you may find that we don't appear at all in the top 10, but we do appear in the top ten results in **yahoo.co.uk**.

So what are the factors that have an effect on the result that you get and what is it that accounts for this disparity in results? Well, they include your domain name, how many people follow the link, the content of the website, the headings that you use on your pages, who links to you and how highly they are ranked in turn, the type of files that your website uses, whether you get lots of return visitors or not; and the list goes on with new elements being added almost daily. This can lead to what some call the Google Dance, which is where the rankings are altered according to the change in weighting that is given to the various elements of the algorithm. Just because you are number one now, doesn't mean to say you will be number one tomorrow!

48. All about keywords and metatags

A metatag is something that developed out of managing library books. It is a small piece of information that describes something about the page of a website that the visitor is looking at. At one time, metatags ruled the search engines but this has changed over the years because of abuse by spammers. Nevertheless, they still have their uses and they can still be very helpful when describing your website to search engines. For instance, if you do a search on Google, you will often see a link, followed by a little bit of text about the site - this often comes from the description metatag. You can use metatags to establish copyright or authorship as well as a whole host of other things. There are many different metatags available and I have included more information about them on the website for you.

A keyword however, is a word that the search engines use to determine what your website is all about, so *'gerbil'* would be a key word, but *'and'* wouldn't. You can use keywords in your metatags, but you will also use them in the main body of text and on any given page on the site. Keywords are important when optimising your site for search engines, as I realised when I was trying to figure out why Google didn't like me using the words Womb or Uterus in my Google Ads; after all a hysterectomy is the removal of the womb (also called the uterus) so what was the problem? The problem, it turned out, was that I expected the Google database to be intelligent. It didn't know that the words womb, uterus and hysterectomy were all related, and I had not made it obvious by using all of those words as major keywords, on the home page where they would have the most impact.

A keyword will also help you to spot what might work for your users. Let's face it, most of them will come to you via the search engines initially and you need to have a good idea of what words and phrases they might use to find you with. This is probably not an exercise you should do on your own (because more heads are better than one) so why not get staff, colleagues, friends and family involved too. You never know they may just give you an idea that makes all the difference. So, put up a big sheet of paper somewhere handy and invite everyone to write down the search terms they would use to try to find the product, information or service you are hoping to sell.

Incidentally, there are also tools that you can use to help you drill down through the layers of keywords and phrases. They are often used for helping to construct ads but they can also help give you an idea of what people actually search for when they are looking for someone like you. Where can you find them? On the website of course and I have generated a list of the better ones in the resources section of the website.

49. Keywords

As I have discussed already in the book so far, the key to getting a good ranking on the search engines is to have lots of relevant information about the search term that people are looking for. Relevant information though, means different things to different people and it may be worth having a think about the sorts of keywords your customers might use and then incorporating them into the pages and paragraphs you create about your product and service.

To give you an idea of what I mean, I have listed just some of the keywords and phrases that might be relevant to The Hysterectomy Association, excluding the one we are almost always searched on 'hysterectomy'.

hysterectomy recovery	abdominal hysterectomy	a hysterectomy
recovery hysterectomy	complete hysterectomy	happy hysterectomy
sex after hysterectomy	effects of hysterectomy	having a hysterectomy
surgical menopause	full hysterectomy	hysterectomy association
abdominal hysterectomy recovery	hysterectomy alternative	hysterectomy help
after a hysterectomy	hysterectomy info	hysterectomy society
after hysterectomy	hysterectomy operation	hysterectomy support
bleeding after hysterectomy	hysterectomy procedure	hysterectomy uk
emergency hysterectomy	hysterectomy risk	hysterectomy women
exercise after hysterectomy	hysterectomy surgery	hysterectomy forum
following hysterectomy	keyhole hysterectomy	www hysterectomy
had a hysterectomy	of hysterectomy	life after hysterectomy
hrt after hysterectomy	op hysterectomy	menopause after hysterectomy
hysterectomy after	partial hysterectomy	pain after hysterectomy
hysterectomy and hrt	pros and cons of hysterectomy	post hysterectomy
hysterectomy and weight gain	radical hysterectomy	pregnancy after hysterectomy
hysterectomy and weight	sub total hysterectomy	recovering from
	subtotal hysterectomy	

loss	supracervical hysterectomy	hysterectomy
hysterectomy bleeding	surgery hysterectomy	recovery time after
hysterectomy complication	total abdominal	hysterectomy
hysterectomy complications	hysterectomy	side effects of hysterectomy
hysterectomy depression	total hysterectomy	smear after hysterectomy
hysterectomy faq	type of hysterectomy	vaginal bleeding after
hysterectomy hrt	vaginal hysterectomy	hysterectomy
hysterectomy post op	what is a hysterectomy	weight gain after
hysterectomy recovery time	hysrectomy	hysteretomy

All of the words and phrases are those that women use to try and find us - including the misspellings. So, why not get your notepad out, sit down with the pen and get thinking about all the different words that people might use for your product or service.

If you are having problems thinking of the words and phrases people might use, you could try the free keyword tool that the nice people from Google provide; you can find it at **adwords.google.com/select/KeywordToolExternal**. This handy little utility allows you to find out what people are searching for and gives a guide as to how many people are using those words as keywords for their advertising programmes, although it won't give you actual costs or numbers.

50. Search engine submission

A search engine is simply a database which contains the details of websites. Contrary to some peoples' belief they don't go and search the whole web when they are trying to return a result for you, they simply search their own databases - although their databases do have many millions of entries in them. What this means is that submitting your website to a search engine can be a bit of a hit and miss affair. You give them your web address usually via a nice little form, with a little bit of information about your site and eventually they will send along their automatic 'spider' to index your web pages. If you are linked to by any other website that is regularly '*spidered*' then your site will be picked up this way as well.

On most search engines there will also be a link on the home page (often at the bottom) that says something along the lines of 'submit your site'. Just follow the links and complete the information to the best of your ability.

There is also software you can buy, or online services you can use, that will submit your site to 100's, if not 1000's of search engines and directories. They can be a bit of a curate's egg and could even cause you problems, particularly if you use several of them or are also submitting the site yourself in tandem. This is because the search engine automated systems may think you are trying to spam them (trying to create multiple entries to trick the search engine into giving you a higher ranking) and they may then prevent you from registering at all or even remove you from the index.

You also need to be aware that different search engines require different information to create an entry, which means that any tool you use must be capable of dealing with this. And finally, some search engines may charge you a fee even to look at your site, but payment of the fee doesn't guarantee that they will index you either - figure that one out if you can!

51. Undoing the reciprocal link myth

A reciprocal link occurs when two websites link to each other by mutual agreement. In theory, the search engines love sites that link to one another; it helps them to ascertain which ones have value, because the search engine developers reason that sites wouldn't link to your site if it wasn't relevant would they?

So there-in lies the question, would a site link to you if yours wasn't good or even relevant to their subject matter? And the answer has to be '**yes**', in some instances they would if you provided a reciprocal link back to them or if you paid them. The premise is that the more sites you have linking to your own, the higher a ranking you will get on the search engines. And this was true until very recently when those search engine boffins realised that links between one website and another wasn't necessarily an indicator of relevance or value. So, whilst they are still good to have, they no longer have the same degree of importance within the algorithms that the search engines use to determine which sites they will display for any given search term.

However, as with everything else in this book, there are exceptions to the rule and the exception in this instance is when a large and well-placed site links to you. The reason this happens is that they rate your information so highly that they are prepared to provide you with a link. So if you are lucky enough to get one of the bigger Internet players such as Amazon, Ebay or the BBC linking to you, then your relevance is magnified as far as the search engines are concerned. I am lucky enough to have, not only the BBC, Amazon and a number of the large health sites providing links back to the site, but also the NHS

(National Health Service) which has given the site increased cachet and, therefore, relevance as far as the search engines are concerned.

Of course, there is a tried and trusted way to get a good quality link to your website, which is both relevant (for the search engines) and appropriate (to the subject of the website). You can do it by crafting a well thought out reply to a question that has appeared within an appropriate discussion topic. Your answer may include a link back to an article, or page, on your website if it helps to explain or expand on your answer.

One word of caution though; in the last year software has been released which allows you to put your website link into a robot which will automatically register you on as many Internet forums as possible. Please let me urge you **NOT** to use this software: I have to deal with the repercussions of it every day of the year when I delete '*new members*' who are listing very dodgy porn sites. And I can assure you that it definitely doesn't boost your rankings on the search engines, mainly because they compare the relevancy of the sites listed in the member registrations with the main content of the website; but also because many forums aren't able to be indexed by the search engines as the web addresses that entries on the forum produce aren't static.

52. Questions of quality

Quality is all in the eye of the beholder; what looks like the most fantastic piece of art deco studio glass to you, might look like something to hand in to the charity shop as soon as possible to me; for instance, my husband loves antiques and I have a passion for Ikea which creates very interesting discussions when we are planning a new room layout or furniture.

But how does this little truism affect you and your online business? Well, it's all down to the customer, and by knowing your current customers requirements, you have a better chance of offering future customers what they might like to buy.

The quality of your offering is demonstrated by all sorts of things; for instance you can easily spot the difference between a baby's first book and an adult classic; or an amateur website and a professional one. Equally, how you present your product tells the purchaser something about the quality, it's not for nothing that expensive perfumes come in elaborate packaging. For your customers, it could be that the price is important; it may be that it is very exclusive or that they can't get the information easily from anywhere else, or you may have received endorsements showing you are well respected in your field. Identify what makes yours a quality product in the eye of your customer, and you have the path to riches my friend.

53. Content vs design

There has long been a debate over whether content (information) is more important than design (the look of the website that presents the information). Being an information scientist and business analyst for my sins, I am of course going to say the quality of information is the key. However, I would also admit that design comes a very close second because it is important for website users to like what they see and be able to find what they are looking for easily as well.

Having said all that though, there are some independent arbiters of what makes a good website! I am talking about the search engines of course, those huge databases that list the myriad of sites that exist for every conceivable topic. Search engines love information; they love 'content' as this is what they base their recommendations on when they return a list of results to a user. There is no reason in the world, why you cannot sell products and have lots of information as well because it all comes down to relevance at the end of the day. By having lots of relevant, timely and useful information on your site you stand a good chance of keeping a visitor interested long enough for them to become a customer as well.

For instance, you could type in the word 'books' into a search engine and I will bet that Amazon comes out somewhere in the top ten of natural search results. This isn't because it has paid to be there, it is because it is full of information about books. Can you do the same with your website? The Hysterectomy Association is essentially an information website with added functionality in the form of a community of users that daily increases the amount of 'information' that the website offers.

Why not try this little exercise out:

- Go to **www.ranking.com** and type in the following web address: **www.hysterectomy-association.org.uk**, you will the see the overall ranking of the site in the context of every other site on the web. Click on the *'more information'* tab and this will give you more information about the site.
- Return to **ranking.com** and type in this web address instead: **www.your-hysterectomy.com,** I suspect you will probably find that it isn't even listed.

Most of the visitors to the first site go there because of its' ranking in the natural search results, whilst the visitors to the second are being driven there by an online advertising campaign. What is the difference between the two? Have a look at both sites and you will see that one is a fully functional website with lots of information and a community, whilst the other is a simple site with only two options, to either buy a book or to sign-up for email hints and tips. I don't think I need to tell you which one the search engines prefer when it comes to information.

54. Free content

When you need to create information for your website you might do a variety of different tasks, such as searching for the latest news about your favourite topic or writing new pages. However, there is a way to ease a small part of your task that is completely free of charge. I am talking about RSS (Really Simple Syndication) feeds. Syndicated content is something that was used exclusively by the news networks. A freelance journalist would find a story; she would write it up and then offer it to an organisation like Reuters who would then syndicate it worldwide. In order to buy this news story from Reuters the big network news agencies would need to spend huge sums of money every month in subscriptions.

Then along came the web and everything changed, not immediately of course, but fairly soon after it all started. Now you can grab a newsfeed for almost any topic you can imagine and add them to your website just like Reuters does. Your visitors get to see something fresh every time they visit and the search engines love you (almost - they don't have a heart .... yet!).

To see how it all works, why not visit the Grow A Better Business website and click on the Latest Business News link which displays a newsfeed from Yahoo! that is updated on an hourly basis. Of course, you may need to do some tweaking with your website as RSS feeds do not automatically work in any web page. Just one word of caution; do make sure that the newsfeeds you choose are **relevant** to your own information; otherwise all your hard-work may be for nought.

You might also be tempted to create a website that comprises just newsfeeds, and there is software that will help you do this, but do bear in mind that although your site would have fresh content, it isn't your own unique content and as a result the search engines won't rate it as highly as the originating source. Therefore, a mix of newsfeeds and unique content written by you is optimum.

55. What's the headline?

A good headline attracts attention. If you don't believe me, next time you are in your local newsagents just scan the shelves and spot which magazines and newspapers are attractive to you. I will almost guarantee it will be something to do with the front-page headline. As hubby says "Dog Bites Postman" just doesn't cut it, but "Postman Bites Dog" just might!

What are the headlines that you use for your business? Are they functional such as 'Improving Your Dog's Behaviour' or do they get people thinking with a headline like 'Does Your Dog Need Braces?'. I can tell you that a good title makes all the difference. Take *101 Handy Hints for a Happy Hysterectomy* as an example. It is upbeat; it lets you know that you will get lots of information from it that might just make a difference and it shows that the operation can be positive, when all the reader may have heard so far is negative. As a result, it outsells my other women's health books by about 10:1. I get lots of feedback about it which is almost all overwhelmingly positive and purchasers will often go on to buy other items from me after getting it, including the other books.

So think of the headline; make it relevant to your keywords and then twist it a little to make people think - it may well buy you a little extra time to convince them that they really do need to get those dog braces after all.

56. Viral marketing

I can assure you that you won't be picking up a dose of bird flu or any other nasty illness that is going to destroy your health for the next 24 hours just by reading this hint. However, there is a similarity though, as viral marketing does act a little like a cold virus because it can spread a message across the Internet very quickly.

You may remember a film called The Blair Witch project. If you do or if you went to see it then you may well have heard about it because of a very successful viral marketing campaign. The campaign suggested that this was a real life film taken by some friends who were out exploring in a forest who then disappeared; no one ever knew what happened to them as only the camera was ever found. As a result the campaign created a huge amount of interest in the film, which subsequently went on to become an unexpected box office hit even though it had cost peanuts (by comparison to most films these days) to make.

There have also been a number of new bands who have erupted on to the music scene that promoted their music on a **myspace.com** website and who are now hitting the big time as a result of all the emails their fans sent to friends.

You may not have the money for a film and you may have the singing ability of your neighbour's cat at midnight, but anyone can create a viral marketing campaign. One of the best ones I came across last year was a telephone conversation about a man ordering pizza. The campaign was created by the American Civil Liberties Union to show just how much our privacy is being invaded and you can have a listen yourself at *www.aclu.org/pizza*.

So, could you think of an angle, produce a short video clip on your mobile phone, show an example of your photographic skills or record your voice on the computer? If so, then you have the makings of your first Internet viral marketing campaign. A good campaign has to have a point to it, it should have a strong call to action or a purpose to it that teaches something; it might be a music download or film clip, an online game, quiz or a free sample. Above all though, it must have a link back to your website otherwise it is likely to end up as just one more deleted email!

57. The rules of attraction

Have you ever really paid attention to what you do when you are on the Internet? It might be time to think about doing so, because your behaviour and the way you search for information can be very relevant when you try to work out what your potential customers might be thinking about when they find you. Notice how quickly you do a search on say Google, Altavista or Yahoo! and when you follow a link, how long do you stay on the site before you hit the back button to try the next one? What were you hoping to find on that page? How many, and what, words do you use when you want to find something? Do you know what you are expecting when you go to a site that you have never visited before; and have you ever really thought about what makes a website easy for **YOU** to use?

Get onto the Web and think quickly (just as your customer might do) about how you would search for the product or service you are planning to offer. What words might you use, are there any relevant phrases or acronyms that customers may use? How did you find out about it originally, why are you interested in it? Pay attention to how long you stay on your competitor's sites, what was it that made you click the back button immediately or that captured your attention so much? What are they doing wrong that you could do better?

You only have a few seconds to make a good impression on the web before that potential purchaser hits the back button. When someone gets to a website, they expect to be able to find what they want quickly and easily. They do not expect to drill down through layer after layer to try to find the gold. There is a common design rule that says you should only make a visitor click three times before they get to what they are looking for. As a result, planning the structure of the information is crucial when making it easy to use. It will pay dividends in the future and you can only do the planning if know the answer to those questions.

58. Up-selling techniques

Have you ever been into a burger bar, placed your order and then been asked, "Would you like fries with that?" If you have, you have experienced up-selling. Up-selling, is a technique that sales staff use to increase the amount that you purchase when you reach the counter. Three for the price of two is another up-selling technique as is suggesting a larger size cola or the very latest version of software.

Is there anything you can do to use up-selling techniques in your online venture? These might include offering portable speakers at reduced cost with the iPod you are selling or maybe you could offer them a slower selling green jumper for half price when they buy the faster selling, full-price red one.

As you travel the web, have a look to see if you can spot how other sites do it and then think about how you might emulate those techniques to up-sell to your customers?

- What about a 'three for the price of two' banner advert.
- You might suggest that spending an extra £5 results in free shipping.
- You could offer them a discount on their next purchase or appointment.

59. Optimising for search

Search Engine Optimisation (SEO) has changed beyond all belief over the last few years. When the web first started it was enough to incorporate a good page title, and your 250 best keywords (only joking about the 250 keywords by the way as that would be enough to get you banned from most search engines). Those heady days have long gone, although many websites still hang on to the outdated notions that this is what SEO is all about. The reason this change came about was the massive abuse of metatags that ensured search results pointed to anything other than sites relevant to the information that the searcher was looking for, thus giving search engines a poor reputation at the time.

Nowadays SEO is all about how you create and present the actual content of a website, the words you use, how those words are presented (in natural language form such as 'the cat sat on the mat' rather than 'cat, cat, cat'), the number, and quality of links coming from other sites and the phrases those sites use as the text to create their link. Therefore, a link to your site from their main body of text has greater value to a search engine than a link that is simply in a list of links on one side of a page.

The sort of HTML that the keywords appear in is also crucial, so a title with the word 'Alien Autopsy' in would have a slightly greater weighting than the words 'alien autopsy' in the body of an article. How the web page in question is structured is also very important, with the top of the page being of greater value to the search engines than the bottom of the page, which is why it can be very important to separate your content from the site's design with a content management system (this is because a lot of the 'coding' that describes how to layout a page is often done at the top). Other important factors include the type of URL's (web addresses) that the site uses for its pages, the titles of individual pages and the way the site is structured. Why not have a look at the website for more on Search Engine Optimisation including links to some of the best online tutorials available.

60. Mailing lists

One of the best ways to build a business on the Internet is by using an email list. Not just including anyone's email address though, but the email addresses of people who are already interested in what you do. If you have someone's email address then you can send them information about your products and services as often as you might like to, as long as they have opted in to receiving them.

But how do you get such a mailing list when you are just starting out? Well you could buy them, but I wouldn't really recommend this route because the information may be gathered illegally and you could risk alienating 1000's of people who think you are simply sending them spam, as well as being banned by your Internet Service Provider and website host.

A far more effective method is to create your own by capturing the email address of everyone that has ever contacted you, of course this will take much longer, but it will be worth it's weight in gold. The easiest way to gather this information is to ask people to give it to you, in return for something else. For instance you may send out a regular newsletter or have a white paper on a subject they may be interested in. You might send them a free sample of your music or artwork, or perhaps a voucher they can use in your shop or for a free consultation. However, if you are gathering personal information in this way, then you do need to be sure that you abide by any data protection legislation that applies in your country. For instance, in the UK you are required to ensure that people can remove their details if they wish.

The final way to use mailing lists is to work with someone that already has one related to the subject area you are interested in. Remember though, that there must be something in it for the person or business providing the list such as a percentage of the profits you make from sales perhaps. This type of activity is called Joint Ventures, and there is a little more information about it in the section on Tools and Techniques.

61. PPC marketing

PPC stands for *'Pay per Click'* and it is one of the oldest ways of generating revenue to be found on the Internet. Let's assume that you have a website and you have a number of banner and text adverts displayed; with PPC every time a visitor to your website clicks on one of these adverts the owners of the adverts will be charged a small fee and you will receive a proportion of that revenue.

In the example above, you can see my advert in the right hand column, it is the second one down. When someone clicks on that advert they are taken to a page on my website that sells a book.

In this example, I used the search term *'hysterectomy recovery'* and my advert was shown because that is one of the keyword phrases that triggers this particular ad to display. In January 2008, I paid 3p for every click on instances of that advert that were triggered on Google with the keyword *'hysterectomy recovery'*. That key word was searched for 2911 times in the same month and 303 of those searchers clicked on the advert, meaning it had a click through rate of 10.4%, which is excellent. My total bill in January, for all the adverts and keywords was £75.00 and, because I track what customers do on my website, I know that I made many times more than this cost back in sales.

It is up to you how you integrate PPC marketing into your website, but if you don't want to set up a scheme yourself then you might use something like Google Adsense on your site or work with Adbrite instead to provide the banners for you. There is more about both of these services in the Tools and Techniques section.

Nevertheless, if you did want to do it yourself, then content management software can sometimes include a way of managing such advertising campaigns. You would recruit your advertisers directly, set your own price for clicks and/or impressions, then send out the monthly invoices based on either the number of impressions (times their advert was shown to a visitor) or the number of times visitors clicked the advert. This way does of course involve more work on your part - but you will not be sharing the profit with an intermediary either. On the other hand, the big Internet wide systems may be able to attract advertisers you could not hope to get on your own.

It might be worth finding out whether PPC marketing works for your website by using Google or Adbrite first: if they prove successful you could then start to incorporate your own system as well if you wanted to.

62. Just say 'Thanks'

A simple 'thank you' goes a long way in helping to create successful customer/client relationships. On the bottom of every invoice I send out in the post is a short, hand written note that says "*thank you for your order, it is very much appreciated*". This is because I do appreciate every order, no matter what the value. Anyway, to say 'Thank You' costs nothing and goes a long way to making your customers feel valued and appreciated for themselves, not just for their wallets.

You can even do it by email as well. Once an order has been placed on line, whatever the order is for, you could send an email saying thank-you and giving your customer some more information about how their order will be handled, when you might ship it to them or how to download it, if it is digital. You might also decide to take this opportunity to up-sell to them, perhaps offering them a discount at the same time because they are now a valued customer.

Monetizing the Internet

Dave's brilliant idea for DIY money trees had really paid off!
(© Photographer: Iryna Bodnaruk | Agency: Dreamstime.com)

I don't know why you're in business, but I can take a guess that it probably has something to do with earning money! The Internet is a great enabler, it provides you with the opportunity to approach people you might never get through the office door and into markets you might never have thought of, but guess what .... it also allows you to make money in many other ways too; and this section of the book will take a look at some of the more popular.

63. Affiliate schemes

An affiliate scheme is something that enables you to promote a product you like in whatever way you feel is most appropriate (depending on the agreement you have with the originating website) and in return you receive a commission when a person you have referred does something (such as buy a product or fill in a form).

You can see these schemes on many different websites. Look for a link that may be called something like 'affiliates' or 'partners'; you will often find them in the small print at the bottom of a page. To join, you need provide a few details about yourself, such as your name, contact details, a username and password; and you are away. They will usually pay you by cheque or into a PayPal account. Sometimes they may pay into your bank account directly - Amazon does this for instance. A good affiliate scheme will provide you with lots of tools to help you with your advertising and marketing such as text links and banner adverts for their products or services.

If you are good at marketing, it is possible to develop an excellent second income through affiliate marketing. Of course, some affiliate schemes are better than others are and these will be those providing a quality product that is closely allied to the sort of information you are providing. Therefore, the things I would consider providing to users of the hysterectomy association might be books on the menopause, women's health issues or hormone replacement therapy - because these are the things that my visitors are going to be most interested in. You may also need to think sensitively about the sort of things you promote, for instance, it would not be fair of me to promote children's clothing on a site about hysterectomy and there would be very little point as I could also alienate my web community.

However, as with everything on the Internet, making money from affiliate schemes requires tenacity and dedication. You will need to monitor how well the various programmes you choose are doing and modify or change them as necessary.

64. Swap sites

It may not always be necessary to sell things to establish a business on the Internet. For instance, you could do what Kyle MacDonald did and swap your way to home ownership. Kyle started out with one red paperclip, yes really, and you can read all about him at his blog **oneredpaperclip.blogspot.com**

Now it may not be possible to do the same thing as Kyle anymore as he had the advantage of being 'first to market' with his idea. As a result, he received loads of column inches in the press that helped to spread the popularity of his blog, and eventually get the house he wanted, but it is possible that swap sites will be just what you are looking for, especially if you are starting out a bit strapped for cash.

You may want someone to design a website for you, or help you write some articles, produce a book or even do your accounts; and you could offer some free products or your skills in return. You may even be able to make some money by using a swap site that allows you to sell as well. I've listed a few of the sites that are available on the website.

Here in Dorset, we also have a scheme called Dorchester LETS, which is a community of like-minded people who swap their skills, abilities and time for services and other products, you can find out more about them at the website: **www.dorchester-lets.co.uk**.

65. Banner ads

If you have ever used the World Wide Web, you will have seen a banner advert. They often appear at the top of a web page and are maybe about half the page in width. They will be interactive, in other words, if you click on them they will take you away from the site that you are currently browsing and onto another site. There has been a lot of discussion about whether banner ads work (for advertisers that is) these days. The argument against them is that all Internet users are aware of them and so are able to ignore them. However, if that were the case why would the big guns still be paying for them? As far as I am concerned, they do work but only if a great deal of thought has gone into how they function in the context of a particular website.

So what makes a good banner ad? I suppose the most important element is that its message is allied to the content of the site that it resides on. Therefore, an advert promoting the latest hip-hop band might not work as well on a website that is talking about how to manage your pension!

They also require a strong call to action (telling the reader what to do next) such as *"click here to find out more about managing your pension"*. Whilst this is not fancy, it is straight to the point and there is no ambiguity about what the person is going to get if they click on the link. Do bear in mind that if the advert takes a reader to a porn site instead, your visitor will probably never return to your website again either.

There are only two ways to run a banner ad campaign on a website. Firstly, there are ones you set up and manage yourself. You tout for business from companies that you feel might benefit from advertising on your site; you might create the banners or they could. When you manage it yourself you will check the number of times each banner is presented to your web audience and the number of times one of those visitors clicks on it and then you bill your advertiser at the rate you have negotiated.

The alternative way of managing banner ad campaigns is to work with the likes of Google Adsense or Adbrite. They will provide you with adverts that should match the information that your customers are seeing on the web page they are viewing. However, you are limited in some of your choices about the adverts you show, although they both give you the opportunity to disqualify certain companies or adverts, especially those that might be your competitors.

A well thought out banner campaign can be used to make money for you on your website, but it could also be a major source of visitors to your own website. Why not contact a few sites that you think may have similar subjects to your own and find out whether they might be prepared to let you advertise with them.

66. E-books

An e-book is a book that is delivered to the customer in digital format; it is downloaded from a web page or attached to an email. This book, for instance, is available in e-book form as well as in paperback and I find it fascinating that so many of the big name fiction authors are now starting to publish e-books as well.

All sorts of books can be made into e-books and I've suggested a few below. Why not have a look at some of your own work to see if you have anything that might be suitable too.

▪ Paperback books	▪ Training manuals
▪ Hardcover books	▪ Course outlines
▪ Comic books	▪ Photo Books
▪ Dissertations	▪ Wedding Books
▪ Cookbooks	▪ Calendars
▪ Product Manuals	▪ Portfolios
▪ Sales Proposals	▪ Brochures
▪ Travel Guides	▪ Yearbooks
▪ Presentations	▪ Annual reports
▪ Textbooks	▪ Discussion Documents

As you can see, they don't necessarily need to be limited to a fiction or non-fiction book. They can be given away free or sold and you might even use the format to create a document to tempt visitors to give you their contact details.

So what are the advantages of publishing in e-book form:-

- you have no books to print and then store

- no post and packaging costs to be passed on to the customer
- no publisher to find
- instant delivery to the customer
- no printing costs for the author/publisher that is

Are there any disadvantages? Well of course there are and I have listed a few here:

- the author may lack perceived 'authority' by the customer - because a publishing company hasn't promoted it
- the customer must print it out themselves, which involves time and paper costs they might not have factored into the overall price
- it requires a fair degree of technical knowledge and understanding about how to download an e-book on the part of the customer
- customers have to understand the jargon, *'download'* springs to mind with this one and it may sound more difficult to do than it actually is.
- you don't have the advantage of a big publishing house doing the marketing for you
- If you don't have an editor, how will you know whether your work is good?

Each of these factors, both positive and negative, needs to be carefully considered before embarking on an e-book project, because it can be so easy to make a mistake. It is easy to produce an e-book, therefore it can seem as if everyone is doing it, and of course there are good books and bad books (just as in print publishing) the difference is that it can be harder to tell the wheat from the chaff for the customer. Moreover, just because it is easy does not necessarily mean you should do it. Consider these questions before you start:

- Do I have something worthwhile to share?
- Do I have the knowledge necessary or the research skills to be able to get the best information for my readers?
- Do I have the word processing and computing skills to produce the book?
- Is there someone around I trust enough to act as an informal editor?
- Will my friends, colleagues, partner tell me what they really think or simply say what I want to hear?

If you are still certain you want to go on, then it can be a rewarding occupation - I should know; I've written four now, including this one. However do consider your readers carefully; I am a great bookworm, I love nothing better than getting a brand new paperback, feeling the cover, smelling the print and slowly letting myself get immersed in the story. Personally an e-book just doesn't do it for me and I have to print them out as I find them difficult to read on the computer. This reason alone is why I also offer my e-books as paperbacks.

All of my books ('e' or otherwise) also have an ISBN (International Standard Book Numbering) number as well, since this helps to protect my copyright as well as offering the advantage that the books are then listed on Global Books in Print, which is the booksellers bible. However, not all e-book projects would need to use an ISBN number; I suppose a good rule of thumb would be that if you thought it, or something similar could sell on Amazon, then you will need an ISBN number.

67. The power of a community

A community is a powerful thing and it goes without saying that whatever you are doing on the Internet, especially if you are hoping to run a website to support your venture, then creating a community of users is one of the most powerful things you can do. You only have to look at the forums on The Hysterectomy Association website to see what I mean.

Hysterectomy			
Forum	**Topics**	**Posts**	**Last Post**
Alternatives to Hysterectomy Here you can find out more about possible alternative treatments for your condition.	113	835	Mon Apr 07, 2008 10:27 am SalSilver
Childlessness and Hysterectomy A hysterectomy is a defining moment in many womens lives particularly for those who are still of child bearing age.	68	757	Thu Apr 10, 2008 9:28 am junek
Complications after hysterectomy Whilst the vast majority of hysterectomies are performed without a problem, there are a number that do cause an ongoing problem for women.	501	3859	Fri Apr 11, 2008 9:12 am dibbs99
Life After Hysterectomy There is life after a hysterectomy, it may include the menopause. However, this is not necessarily 'a bad thing' and is perfectly natural. You can post your questions on life, the universe and everything here!	705	6447	Fri Apr 11, 2008 8:47 am loveskeithurban
Conditions leading to Hysterectomy More about the conditions that may result in a hysterectomy. These include endometriosis, cancer, heavy bleeding, pelvic inflammatory disease, fibroids, prolapse of the uterus and complications after childbirth.	423	3726	Fri Apr 11, 2008 6:08 am lisaedu
General Hysterectomy Please use this forum to post enquiries that don't fit any other available category.	1053	9669	Thu Apr 10, 2008 1:18 pm maxine 47
Health Before, and Recovery after, Hysterectomy Use this forum to find out how other women are getting fit before and after their operation.	1623	18348	Fri Apr 11, 2008 6:09 am lisaedu
Men and Hysterectomies Men who are in relationships with women often need information and support as well. This forum can help you to ask for what you need.	16	120	Thu Apr 10, 2008 4:56 am jazz70

If you do go ahead, then the people that get involved in your community will be some of your best supporters; they will be your evangelists (usually!) and may even act as unofficial PA's for you. They will promote your products through their comments because they believe in what you are doing. The community of women that support The Hysterectomy Association is phenomenal; they promote the website to their doctors and local hospitals; they recommend the books to other women facing surgery, but above all they support one another with their own hints and tips on what has worked (or not) for them.

As well as being a fantastic resource, a really great and helpful community on your website will help you to increase the amount of traffic you get from the search engines. They like sites that are 'sticky', that is sites that people spend a lot of time on. In addition, they love sites that people keep going back to.

However, you don't build a community simply by selling a book or a product, your website has to have something extra. You may remember from communities or clubs you are part of yourself that the people in them share a common bond, whether it was improving their chess game, promoting their business or supporting an environmental cause. Online communities work in much the same way but are usually centred around the opportunity to discuss a topic, whether that is via forums, a chat room or by allowing your users to leave comments on articles.

When you start an online community, you may have to do quite a lot of work yourself to get it going; replying to questions and comments takes time and commitment, and you may need to get the ball rolling by asking, and answering, some of your own. In time though, the users take over and you can take more of a back seat, only getting involved if things get heated.

Adding a community element to your website does not have to be difficult as there are many free or paid-for resources available to try. However, one word of caution once you start a community **do not change the way you set it up** (except to update software). I found this out the hard way and ended up losing 1000's of members and archives simply because I had not put appropriate software in place when I began The Hysterectomy Association community elements. 'Be prepared' is the phrase that pays when it comes to community building.

If you want to see just how well community sites can promote a venture visit ***myspace.com*** and have a look at some of the musicians that are now using it to promote themselves. Some of the latest bands have become famous simply because they had such a big community surrounding them on the Internet. If you are planning on targeting the younger generation then finding out how myspace and similar communities work could be your greatest piece of research.

And of course, if you have users that are talking to each other as well as to you, you are getting more and more traffic to your site, which also helps to push it further up the rankings on the search engines. There are literally hundreds of software solutions available for each of the community elements possible, some are free (but that doesn't mean they aren't any good), some are paid for; and in many cases they may also come bundled with the hosting package that you purchased for your website. If this latter is the case you don't have to install anything or configure files or worry about any of the techy stuff - you just need to get on and create a buzz that will encourage people to come back and keep on interacting with each other.

For an idea of how they work, and to see them in action, why not visit one of my websites, ***www.charlton-down.com*** and click on the *'have your say'* link. This forum is not particularly big, but it will help you to see how it works. It uses freely available software called phpbb, which came bundled with the hosting package for the site.

Finally, do remember that a community isn't always appropriate for every website. They take time to develop, time to grow and can be labour intensive at the front end. But if you have a business or project that is based around the needs of a group of people then you probably shouldn't ignore this very powerful tool.

68. Give people options

Strangely, because I know that you will probably have paid for this book over the Internet, not everyone feels comfortable with giving their credit card details online, which means that although there may be many people who really want your product, they will not buy it unless you give them some alternative ways to pay.

The ability to pay by cheque is always appreciated. If you are nervous about supplying goods before you are certain payment is good then why not ensure your terms and conditions include the fact that you will not be shipping the goods until the cheque has cleared. You will probably need to set up a business bank account to take such payments; but you would want one anyway to deposit your Internet payments into as well. So don't forget to tell people to make cheques out to the business name that is on the bank account. You might also offer them the opportunity to pay by cash (if people are likely to be local to you and can drop it in) or money order/postal order.

Have you thought about a credit card processing machine similar to the ones you get in the shops? With these, you could take payments over the telephone. They are reasonably low cost to run, with a small monthly rental charge and a percentage of each transaction in charges. However, to get one you will need to have that business bank account in place. Remember though that you will need a phone line that is dedicated to the credit card processing machine as you cannot have a conversation with someone and process a credit card at the same time - I know it is obvious when you think about it, but personal experience ensures the need to share this with you.

If you are offering alternative methods of payment, you need to say so - make it obvious to your customers because that can break down one of their biggest objections to buying from you. Include your business account name (for cheques), a telephone number to call and your address so they know where they can post an order form to.

Of course, if you have international customers then they will only have the option of paying online. I don't accept foreign cheques because of the additional cost of clearing them into a sterling bank account. However, if you are likely to process large amounts of foreign transactions then it might be worth investigating alternative currency accounts.

Giving people options like this, is one way of subtly letting them know that you put your customers' needs first.

69. A word about customer service

My mother recently bought a brand new car from her local dealership and the customer care she received was outstanding. Firstly, there was the care and attention paid to the sale process itself - I know I was there! She was contacted a few days before she was to collect the car to make sure that everything was still OK.

On the day itself, she was given an enormous bouquet of flowers to say 'thank-you' and she also received seven days free insurance and went home very happy indeed. In addition, the friend who had recommended her also received a nice cheque for £75 in the post too.

But, that's not all. Every Saturday she can take her car to the dealership and they will clean it for her, while she enjoys complimentary tea, coffee and Danish pastries. Every couple of months the dealership have an event for their customers. One of the most memorable was the Carol Service they arranged at Chester Cathedral.

The thing that really swung it for Mum though, was that they aren't open on Sunday; instead their door hanger says *'at home with the family'*! Just this one thing - without everything else - shows a company that cares, about it's customers and it's staff - can you say the same about your business?

I'll let you into a little secret, the car dealership is called the Mitchell Group and it is based in Ellesmere Port.

Tools and Techniques

Jane found that sticking pins in the bride was the perfect stress reliever!
© Photographer: Carla F. Castagno | Agency: Dreamstime.com

The Internet is awash with all sorts of tools that will help you to build a more effective business. In many cases you can get some of the best almost free of charge; for instance you only pay when something happens as in Google Adwords. Others may cost a little more, but compared to the charges you may expect to have for an office or shop unit, are little more than the proverbial peanuts. The following hints will guide you towards some of the more effective ones.

70. Drop shipping

There is a way of stocking your website, shop or office without needing to physically touch any of the goods you are selling at all. Often called drop-shipping you may have seen it in the physical world with the likes of Avon or other party plan systems. You choose what you want to buy from an 'agent' at a party that takes place in a friends home usually. You make the payment and when the goods arrive at the agent they are delivered to you! They can also come by post directly from the company that has sold it.

Does this exist on the Internet - you bet it does. Cafepress is an example of drop shipping and you can find out a little more about Cafepress in the section on Instant Business Opportunities. In fact there is a whole host of information on the Internet about drop shipping opportunities and some of them are listed on the website.

In fact drop shipping is a great way to extend the products that you offer through your website.

71. White label sales

White label is very similar to drop-shipping except that when the customer gets the goods, the invoice they receive is from you. They have no idea where the goods have actually come from; as far as they are concerned it is from your warehouse off Camden High Street.

One of the advantages of White Label selling is that you can seem to be much bigger than you actually are, you can offer a much larger range of stock than you would otherwise be able to do. As with drop-shipping you simply receive the difference between the wholesale price and your selling price. In some cases, you can even set your own selling prices for the goods.

I have listed a number of white label services on the website. Why not check them out and see if any might fit in with your business.

72. Google adsense

By now, you may be familiar with the term 'Google Adsense' as I have referred to it on occasions within the book. If you are still unsure about what, or who, it is then visit the website and have a look at the home page.

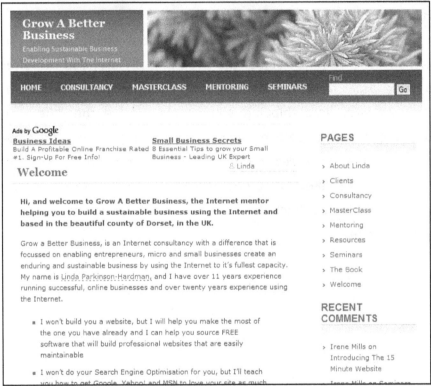

You will see a section at the top, which say *Ads by Google*; this is Google Adsense in operation on a website. Every time someone clicks on one of those adverts, I am paid a little money; how much money I receive depends on how much the businesses that created the ads in the first place has paid Google to have their ads appear, less the commission that Google takes.

Some sites are earning thousands of pounds every month simply from placing Google Adsense on their website in the most prominent positions. Moreover, the visitors that are sent to the websites listed in the adverts are making the expense worthwhile through their subsequent purchases. And, whenever you use the Google search engine, you may also see the same, or similar, adverts displayed at the top and on the right hand side of the search results pages.

The reason Adsense works is that advertisers (like me) agree to pay Google a small amount of money for every advert that someone clicks on in order to have qualified leads driven to their website. It is also contextual which means that your website will only show my adverts if they are relevant to the subject matter of the page that is being displayed to the viewer at any given time.

Google Adsense is completely free to use on your website; you can sign up today by going to: ***www.google.com/adsense*** and registering. When your application has been accepted, you will be given the opportunity to create the types of adverts you would like to appear on your website and you simply copy and paste the text they give you for each type of advert into the place you want it to appear. There is lots of information on the Adsense website that tells you how to do this and I have also included a beginner's guide on the website.

In order to make an income from Google Adsense you will need to have a website or webpage that you are able to edit yourself and to which you can add the Adsense code. You will need to have a little patience as you wait for the Google software to get to grips with the sort of information you have on your website. Adsense seems to work better on sites that have a specific topic/subject/theme or product simply because those sites are more likely to attract (and retain) people interested in that particular interest area.

A lot of research has also gone into where the best advert placements on a web page are, and it seems that the top left hand corner is favourite, closely followed by the top right. And it seems that we are more drawn to links in the text which are often underlined and in blue, although some other web marketing guru's have suggested that links in the text don't work as well as lists of links at the end of an article do. So perhaps placing your Adsense links at the end of an article or web page might be appropriate as well. The beauty of it is, that you can play around with them to see which ones work and which ones don't - because Google allows you to track them as well!

73. Google adwords

Google Adwords is the companion programme to Adsense and is the flip side of the coin. Adwords is the programme that enables a website author to create an advert that shows up when someone searches for a particular term on Google, AND on those websites that are registered for Adsense who have similar, relevant content.

Once again, it is free to join and you can create a new account simply by going to **adwords.google.com**. Bear in mind that this may default to a country prefix like .co.uk if you are not in the US, but it doesn't really matter, as you will be able to have adverts show up all across the web, from one side of the world to the other. Conversely though, if you only have UK based customers you can set it to show your adverts only to those who are searching Google in the United Kingdom.

The Adwords system itself is very simple to use, but can take a long time to master - and it is easy to spend a lot of money not producing any tangible results at all. Why is that I hear you ask? Well to put it simply, you agree with Google (through the software) how much you are prepared to pay them every time someone clicks on one of your advert links regardless of where that link was shown. It is worth bearing in mind that you will pay for every click and your cost per click (CPC) can be as little as a few pence or as much as £1 or two.

How much you pay will depend on a variety of factors which include how good your copy writing skills are, which countries you want the ads to show up in, whether you want them to show up only on the Google search engine or on other peoples sites, how relevant your site is to the adverts you are promoting, what your daily budget is and finally where you want your adverts to appear in the listings. The latter is one of the most important aspects as this really can make a huge difference to your monthly costs.

Many people will tell you that it is vitally important to ensure that your adverts are ranked in the top four, as this means you will always be on the first page of any Google and AOL search (yes that is right, Google powers AOL searches!). Why not go to Google, do a search for your main search term (for me it is usually hysterectomy) and see the adverts on the right hand side of the page. These are what you will be competing against, so the amount you pay will also be dependent to some extent on what the others are paying as well. I say 'to some extent' because if your advert and landing page (or site) is considered by Google to be more relevant than others, then you may well get a higher ranking for a lower price; and why would Google do that... because they want the experience of their users to be one where they always get the most relevant results first, that's why.

You can get a rough idea of how many other sites are advertising against a particular search term by using the links at the bottom of a Google search page to go to all the following pages until you find the same adverts from the first page recurring.

74. Amazon marketplace

Amazon market place gives us all a chance to benefit from Amazon's pre-eminence in the world of online sales as it allows us to sell unwanted stock, used items, refurbished goods and collectables to Amazon's customers. If you hop along to the Amazon website and do a search for the Da Vinci Code, what you may well come across is something like the following:

 The Da Vinci Code by Dan Brown (Paperback - 1 Mar 2004)
Buy new: ~~£6.99~~ **£3.99**   In stock
Used & new from **£0.01**
You save: **£3.00 (43%)**

The bit we are interested in is next to the *'Used & new link'* as this is the link that takes us to Amazon Marketplace, where we will see a list of people/businesses who are selling The Da Vinci Code as well, probably at a far cheaper price than you can buy it from Amazon themselves. You will be able to see that in this example we can get a used copy of the book for as little as 1p (plus post and packaging of course). When you are shown this list, you will be able to check the details of the item, whether it is in good condition or not, have a look at how well the sellers are rated by their customers, where they are based, how long they might take to send the item and then make a decision yourself about whether you want to buy from them or not.

The Marketplace works by allowing sellers to advertise a product they want to sell. If it is sold, Amazon charges a commission to the seller and also charges the purchaser the standard shipping cost, which is then passed to the seller as well. An email is sent to the seller by the Amazon system with details of the sale and to whom they should send their product. You simply package them up and send them off. Every month, Amazon credits your nominated bank account with any earnings you have made through your Marketplace sales.

It is free to join and you can do so by visiting *www.amazon.co.uk*. You can add as many items as you wish to your account. Just remember not to sell them anywhere else first though!

75. Writing for the web

Writing for the web is a skill that is not necessarily learnt easily. When we have something to say, we want to be fulsome and expansive, we want to educate and elucidate and that's great when you are writing a book, a thesis or a report for the managing director. But on the web, it just doesn't work. Jakob Nielsen, the doyen of good website design, has just three rules for writing on the web:

1. Be succinct and write no more than 50% of the text you would have used in a hardcopy publication.

2. Make it easy to scan read as most people will search the text, looking for links to information and other interactive features; they pick out keywords, sentences, and paragraphs that are of interest to them whilst skipping over those parts that they feel are less relevant. Therefore don't insist your visitors have to read long and continuous blocks of text.

3. Use links between pages to split up lengthy information into multiple sections.

Reading on a computer is around 25% slower than reading from paper. Even users who don't know this research fact usually say that they have difficulty reading online text and it gives me a headache and can make me feel nauseous. So I almost always print whatever document I have picked up online. This means that if you have a long document you want to share, create it as a separate document designed for printing and keep the online version to short and manageable chunks of **RELEVANT** information.

It helps if you can keep it to a screen length, although I appreciate this is becoming more difficult with the increasing variety of hand held devices. But you definitely need to ensure that your readers never have to scroll horizontally on a normal computer screen, which means keeping website layouts to a minimum width.

Try writing your text with headings and then use sub-headings if

```
Headline
            Subheading
                    Sub-sub heading
```

you think that they are appropriate; finally, you can also use sub-sub-headings. I am told that nesting headings (see example above) also helps blind users who are using screen reading software, meaning that you also meet one of your legal obligations. And don't forget, a heading should tell the reader what to expect.

You could also use **highlighting** and *emphasis* to make certain words stand out. Finally, don't forget that most links on the web are <u>underlined</u> and in another colour (usually blue), forget this one at your peril.

If you have a long document that you don't want the reader to print out, then creating several pages that are each coherent in themselves makes much more sense and ensures readability. You can add links to the other pages at the top or at the bottom using a relevant heading to allow your readers to determine which sections they would like to read. Try to avoid, however, using the eponymous 'Page Two' as a link, this is neither helpful nor encouraging to a visitor.

76. Online payment systems

First, we had the Internet, and then came the web and later we had the ability to take payments for goods and services over the Internet with a credit or debit card.

When online payments systems first started it could be incredibly difficult to get an account which would allow you to take such payment; the banks were, understandably, wary of the anarchy that the Internet presented to their nice ordered ways of doing business. You had to be well established or have a fabulous business plan which would show how much money you were going to take - at least that was the case before the collapse of the Internet stocks. It was just too difficult for the small trader to take payments for their goods and services.

For a few years, I relied on people printing out an order form and sending me a cheque in the post, if they remembered to send it that is. However, one of the problems with postal ordering is that the momentum for purchase recedes quite quickly and the customer may eventually tear the cheque up and forget all about the book they were hoping to buy.

In addition, many other sites had products that sold for less than £1. The owners didn't want to pay horrendous charges, which could be more than the cost of the goods to the purchaser. However, with the advent of Ebay there had to be a way to allow its users to take payments easily for the things they were selling. So Ebay created PayPal - the first of a number of online payment systems specially designed for small businesses. Such services normally have no sign-up fee and just take a small percentage of each payment to cover the costs of running the service.

Those just starting out on the road to Internet millions and those who are only selling a few of their own products and services, have very simple needs and these systems are the easiest way to take payments that you can find. They are recognised and trusted by millions of people worldwide and the funds that accrue in your account can be credited to your bank account and you can usually receive payments in a variety of currencies, you simply convert them online to allow you to withdraw them to your bank.

To sell something, it is normally a fairly simple job to create a 'buy now' or 'add to cart' button and then copy and paste the code the system creates into the right part of the web page. In fact, you only need a nice picture, a bit of information and a button to get started right away.

77. Shopping cart systems

If you are simply selling a single product or service then you may feel you don't need to read this hint and feel free to skip to the next one in the queue. However, if you have more than one product or service that your visitors may want to purchase, then a shopping cart can reap huge rewards.

A shopping cart allows you to list your products or services in a 'shop front', allowing customers to go along the virtual aisles picking those items they are interested in, adding them to their 'basket' before heading off to the 'checkout' to make their payment. They operate in a very similar way to your local supermarket with the exception that there is no happy smiling face to greet your customer when they reach the end of the queue - in fact there are no queues either.

There are a huge number of shopping cart solutions available, some you install and host yourself, others are hosted for you and some come built in to online payment systems like PayPal. The latter can offer more flexibility and power, but the former are more controllable. They will all link to your chosen payment provider, whether it is PayPal, Nochex, WorldPay or your own bank. And they all offer your customer a three step process.

1. select the goods they want to purchase
2. go to their basket and click make payment
3. complete their payment to finish the transaction

After years of trying out different resources I have finally settled on a hosted cart which offers me a huge range of additional functionality. I now have a service that enables me not only to sell physical items, but stores digital items securely, provides me with my autoresponse service for newsletters, that allows me to track adverts to see how successful they are and finally gives me the opportunity to set up my own affiliate scheme. However, it costs me around £60.00 each month to run, but this is be small potatoes when you think of the costs of running a shop on the high street.

You can have a look at how some of the free online payment systems work in the resources section of the Grow A Better Business website.

78. Create your own affiliate schemes

Your customers can be your best allies - if you have given them a product that they love and find beneficial that is. I know that one of my books '101 Handy Hints for a Happy Hysterectomy' does this, because I get several emails everyday telling me so. Therefore, I have given my customers the opportunity to join in my success by receiving a proportion of the sales revenue I receive whenever someone places an order because they have recommended me.

Affiliate schemes work by giving each member a unique code (a little like a bank account number) that is incorporated into any links that they create to my products and services. Each time someone clicks on one of their links, whether it is in a web page or an email they have sent out, the database records that unique code. Then when the person who followed the link buys something, the member receives a proportion of the sale price.

To create an affiliate scheme for your own users you will need software that allows people to sign up for the scheme and you will need to provide links and banners for all of the products that you want to include. You also need to provide your affiliates with up-to-date statistics about how their campaigns are doing.

You also need to decide whether you will pay an affiliate simply because they direct someone to your website, or only if someone buys something; this decision is really going to depend on your business. You may feel that you get better sales results through your newsletter or autoresponders, therefore it may be in your best interests to pay out to your affiliates whenever someone signs up to receive your emails - this might be the case if you are selling information. Alternatively, if you were selling tangible products such as your own CD recordings then you would probably want to pay out whenever you make a sale from an affiliate's link.

Whichever route you take however, you have to produce results; there is no point in having affiliate schemes if the products you offer don't sell. Your affiliates will go somewhere else instead as they have to invest time and effort into persuading someone to click on a link. Usually products don't sell because they are not 'packaged' attractively enough. What this means is that the place that your affiliate links to on your website has to be attractive to every potential purchaser. Invest some time, and money if necessary, in getting these pages right - believe me you won't regret it because a good landing page will result in high quality affiliates joining your scheme, as well as an increase in sales from the direct visitors as well.

79. Ad tracking software

One of the problems when you are selling things on the Web is that you may not know how people find your site or your advert. As a result, it can be hard to find out which methods of advertising and marketing work for you and which ones don't. A number of solutions have been created to try to deal with this problem and one of the best is some sort of ad tracking software. If you are lucky and you have an interdependent host looking after your shopping cart then you may have it built in to the system and all you will have to do is turn it on.

101 Link From Recovery Page	☐	811	839	137	16.9%	£670.31	96	11.8%
1-After Hysterectomy	☐	7330	9936	911	12.4%	£883.05	118	1.6%
1pg link from information page	☐	41	45	8	19.5%	£18.49	3	7.3%
2-Information	☐	1163	1288	71	6.1%	£162.67	15	1.3%
3-Support	☐	1021	1202	63	6.2%	£204.16	22	2.2%
4-The Hysterectomy Association	☐	28	36	0	0%	£0.00	0	0%
5-Hysterectomy Recovery	☐	63	68	0	0%	£35.00	1	1.6%
Additional Purchase Coupon	☐	469	618	5	1.1%	£1511.52	133	28.4%
Free ebook - Hysterectomies for Men	☐	180	205	0	0%	£25.01	14	7.8%
hints and tips updated 101	☐	133	161	0	0%	£179.77	27	20.3%
hints and tips updated he4m	☐	1	1	0	0%	£0.00	0	0%
hints and tips	☐	1	1	0	0%	£0.00	0	0%

The service I use for the shopping cart on the association website has this capability built in and it has been invaluable in helping me to determine which of my Google ads produce the required results - whether that is sales or people signing up to our hints and tips and downloading our free booklet.

If you are only using Adwords then you could use its built-in analytic tool. Setting this up takes a little time and effort, but it will tell you how successful the various campaigns are - you can see the results from a small portion of one of my campaigns in the right hand three columns in the image above. Of course, it is understood that it will not work with any other pay-per-click advertising you might be doing. Yahoo Search Marketing and Microsoft AdCenter have similar analytic tools, but again they only work with their own adverts.

The way that ad-tracking software works is by placing a small piece of code within the link that visitors click on to get to your page. These can be as general or as specific as you might like and could even be used to tell you how successful individual key words are so that you can fine-tune your Adwords campaigns to the nth degree. When a visitor clicks on the link, they transmit a tiny piece of information to your tracking software that then places a cookie on their browser, which will track what they then do and match everything up at the end of their time on your website. Therefore, it will tell you how many people buy something, what the cost per click is for each advert (divide by the amount spent on the particular product) who signs up for your newsletter as well as a huge variety of other data.

80. Autoresponders

An autoresponder is exactly what it says it is. It responds automatically when someone contacts a specific email address or fills in a particular form and you may well have received them without noticing.

Have you ever sent an email to a company and received the reply that says something like "thank you for contacting us; we would like to assure you that someone will be in touch regarding your query within 24 hours"? If the answer is yes, then that is an autoresponder at work.

Autoresponders are brilliant pieces of software engineering which can mimic real people in the online world and give your venture the appearance of being open 24/7. But they can also do so much more and may even be the extra sales force you need. In fact, you may have bought this book because you signed up for the *Five Day E-course* or if you downloaded one of the free e-books that I give away occasionally. If you did, then you have experienced the power of the autoresponder. In some areas of Internet business, they are used extensively to promote workshops, books, people and software yet in others they are hardly used at all. So if you are hoping to make a killing selling information about how to keep guppies in your bath, then you may do well to offer a free hints and tips service that promotes your book as well as providing potential customers with valuable information.

Autoresponders are also at the heart of the game to capture your visitors email addresses. They give you the chance to set up a booklet to download or series of emails that can be scheduled to go out each day, each week or each month (after someone signs up). You receive a small piece of code when you have set it up which provides you with a form to copy and paste into your web page. You can see an example on the ***www.growabetterbusiness.co.uk*** website of the sort of form you could expect to use, you will find it under the *'five day e-course'* link.

Autoresponder Name	Msgs in Series	Unique Clients	Removes	Total Subscribes	Sharable	Detailed Report	Update Autoresponder
1. Hints and Tips for a Happy Hysterectomy	15	128	15	143	YES	View	Test | Edit | Add Message | Delete
101 Order Follow Up	2	578	49	627	NO	View	Test | Edit | Add Message | Delete
2. Recovery Hints and Tips	15	708	64	772	YES	View	Test | Edit | Add Message | Delete
Free Booklet	5	6079	697	6776	YES	View	Test | Edit | Add Message | Delete
Free Hints & Tips	13	2315	250	2565	YES	View	Test | Edit | Add Message | Delete
Free Hints and Tips - Updated Version	15	444	42	486	YES	View	Test | Edit | Add Message | Delete
Local Group Leaders	8	2	0	2	YES	View	Test | Edit | Add Message | Delete
Order Thank You	2	1356	117	1473	YES	View	Test | Edit | Add Message | Delete
The Hysterectomy Association Newsletter	1	493	26	519	YES	View	Test | Edit | Add Message | Delete

Everyday on the main hysterectomy website, 20 to 30 people sign up for either a free booklet, which has three emails that are sent out over three days (the last one suggesting that they also sign up for our hints and tips), or one of two series of hints and tips - with information for pre-hysterectomy preparation or post-op recovery - that send out one email each day for fifteen days each. This simple exercise, which is all automated, has resulted in a mailing list of around 10,000 people. Every month I send out a newsletter to those people, giving them information about the latest research findings, alternatives to hysterectomy and HRT, additional resources that are available on the website, updates on meetings and workshops that are taking place, as well as promoting one of the items we sell. Not surprisingly, the sales of that one item usually jump in the week following the newsletter.

81. Clickbank

ClickBank is one of the Internet's largest digital market places; you can find all sorts of interesting and useful information, e-books, software and other digital items on it. You will need to use some discretion about what you go for, but that is true of anything on the Internet really isn't it?

However, one of the biggest benefits of ClickBank is the powerful way it leverages other people through affiliate schemes to help sell your products. For instance, you might have bought this book via any one of several ways:- it may be a paperback or the e-book version, you might have picked it up from Amazon in the US or the UK, you could have ordered it direct from Lulu or you may even have found it on ebay; or you could have used ClickBank.

The only difference with ClickBank is that it is entirely possible that someone else sold it to you on my behalf because they liked it so much. In addition, for their belief in my product I share the money I am paid for the e-book with them.

Here is how it works:

- Mr J has recently developed some innovative techniques for shearing sheep and has decided to produce an e-book about them.

- He decides he will add it to ClickBank and decides to charge $10 - (Clickbank only charges in dollars).

- He also decides that he will let ClickBank affiliates earn 50% of the cost if they promote it and it leads to a sale.

- Ms A has bought the book on sheep shearing at ClickBank.

- She likes it so much and thinks that other sheep shearers are going to be so fascinated by the insights it has to offer that she signs up as a reseller of the e-book at ClickBank.

- She has noticed that the cost of the e-book is $10 and that she will get 50% every time someone buys the e-book as a result of clicking on her link; so assuming she can generate enough interest she stands to make $5 every time she helps to sell the e-book

- She puts a link to the e-book on her website in an article about how good it is at explaining all the new ways to shear sheep

- She might even put a link to her article on Google, through Adwords

- She may also send an email out to everyone that has signed up for her sheep shearing hints and tips letting them know about the e-book and giving them a link to where they can buy it.

And so it goes on ... and on ... and on... Assuming that the e-book is a good one, and it gives people the information they need then she will continue to generate an income for as long as the book is available, and she promotes it.

You could even resell the 'e' version of this book yourself if you wanted to, and earn some of the revenue as well. You can visit my website ***growabetterbusiness.co.uk*** to find out how. Don't forget to use the easy steps outlined above to start generating your own income from reselling this e-book. Of course when you have created your own masterpiece don't forget to let me know so that I can do the same in return.

82. ebay

I think I have said earlier in the book that you don't necessarily need a website to use the Internet effectively in business. Ebay is one of the many services which has a huge following and is used to sell anything from antique furniture to Radley handbags and even mud from Glastonbury (don't ask!). You can buy healthy foods, herbal supplements, e-books on every subject under the sun, coal and wood for open fires and even homes these days.

Don't dismiss it as something that you only use to sell your unwanted items on. With ebay stores you can sell your handmade cushions, joinery products, nuts and bolts or even items for aromatherapy massage. The most well known format is the online auction, where people bid on an item of their choosing. I've recently sold an antique dining table, which I put on with an auction format starting at 99p, I set a reserve price which meant it wouldn't be sold too cheaply but would give me a good indication of what the real price might be if it didn't reach that reserve. Fortunately it sold!

The real beauty of ebay however is the system of feedback, which gives the buyer an indication of how well the trader, or purchaser, is thought of by the rest of the community. Sure, this has the ability to be manipulated, but even so it is still a good arbiter of the good and the bad.

In addition to the auction format, you can also sell with a 'buy now' price, which gives people the chance to snap up your bargain without the hassle of sitting through the auction and risking not getting the item they want at the end. Items can be for sale in auction or 'buy now' formats for up to ten days in the UK, but if you have regular stock items then you would probably want to investigate setting up a shop as this will allow you to keep an item available until it is sold; additionally you get lower listing fees as well.   It costs just £6.00 a month to open a basic level shop.

You could even use ebay as your online shopping cart if you wanted to, as it will fit in with any existing website you may have. So if you are a counsellor then you may source, and sell, books on psychotherapy or self help; if you are a carpenter, what about selling your products on ebay as well as through your website? The trick with the Internet is to maximise the exposure your products and services get, and ebay certainly helps you to do this.

83. Wordpress

You may have noticed as you read your way through this book the number of times I have mentioned Wordpress or blogging. There are very many reasons why I recommend Wordpress and use it on various websites that I run and I thought a short list may be helpful:-

- Ease of use, either adding new information or updating information.
- You can try it out free of charge and set one up within five minutes at **wordpress.com**
- You can even use your own web address on wordpress.com
- If you decide to transfer to your own web hosting agreement, you can download the software, set it up on your own space and then copy your database from wordpress.com - easy!

So, those are the pro's, are there any con's? Of course there are, nothing is ever perfect and everything can always be improved.

1. You can't use anything like Google Adsense with the free version at **wordpress.com**. If you want to do so, you will need to set up your own hosting account.
2. It can become very addictive!

84. Publishing online

As you have probably discovered by now, I also run a health information website for women and this website has provided me with much of the experience I am sharing with you in this book. In the course of this work, I have written three books called 101 Handy Hints for a Happy Hysterectomy, The Pocket Guide to Hysterectomy and Losing the Woman Within. The first two have been selling for a few years and are ones I printed myself and now sell directly to the public - incidentally I also supply Amazon! Originally, they were only available as e-books, but there is something special about a physical book and as soon as I started providing paperback versions of the books the sales skyrocketed.

However, although we have in excess of 150,000 visitors each month to the website and a good proportion of those are from outside the UK, I found it hard to make sales of the paperback books outside the UK. Neither could I get them listed on Amazon in the US without using Amazon Advantage, which would see my profits reduced to zero because of the horrendous shipping charges it takes to get stock to the Amazon warehouse in America.

Until I discovered Print On Demand (POD) that is... (ta da ... quick twirl in the 'phone box and emerge looking gorgeous in blue Lycra and a little tiara - hopefully some of you at least will remember Wonder Woman!). What POD has enabled me to do is sell a book anywhere in the world, and supply it within days of the order. The books can be ordered from any online bookstore immediately, including Amazon, Barnes and Noble, WH Smith and even Tesco. When an order is placed, the book is printed and shipped. It is a fantastic way of reducing stock and shipping costs.

What is the catch I can almost hear you cry! There is no catch really except that you don't get the same amount of money for each book sold as you would do if you printed and sold them yourself. Instead, you set a royalty fee for each book you have written and that is what you receive for each copy sold. Of course, neither do you have to process the order, wrap the book up, take it to the post office and then hope it arrives with your customer.

To create a book through a Print on Demand service is normally free as they simply take a percentage of each sale to cover costs. However if you want global distribution that allows your book to appear in online bookstores then you may need to pay an additional fee. If you take the Global Distribution route, you will normally be assigned an ISBN (international standard book numbering) number for your book, and your book will be made available to the Bowker database, which means that any bookseller will be able to find it and sell it if they want to. Bingo!

However, be aware that if you use an overseas POD service that provides an ISBN number for you, then you may well be charged tax on your royalties. If you find yourself in this situation then you need to contact your local tax office for advice.

At the time of writing (although this might have changed by now) 101 Handy Hints for a Happy Hysterectomy is the number one or two listed book when you search for 'hysterectomy' on **Amazon.co.uk** and about number three on **Amazon.com**. All right I know you aren't planning to have one anytime soon sir! But it just goes to show what the combination of having a well visited, and highly respected, website together with global availability, can really do.

85. PR distribution services

By now, you should be clear about one thing, to be successful in business on the web you need to promote your product or service just as you do in the real world. If you don't promote your product or service, you won't sell anything and the web won't work. However and fortunately, life is getting easier by the day for those of us using the Internet to build our business with the latest generation of press release distribution services.

Some services are free to use, some charge and others are a mixture of the two. However, free is not necessarily 'a bad thing' and paid for doesn't necessarily mean that your press release will gain any more column inches than the free services.

What most services allow is for your press release to be picked up by the major search engines (so don't forget to include a link to your website); but you may not be aware that many newspapers and other media services also source information and stories from them - especially when there is a slow news day. Don't despair if your story relates to something very local, remember that people still add their county or town to a search term and local papers are always trying to find something new and different to offer their readers.

Whether your release is picked up will depend, to a large extent on how well it is written. So, to increase the chance of having a story published, do try to make the editors', freelancers', reporters' or journalists' job easier by presenting the release in a format and style that might appeal to them.

1. You might want to think about why you are writing the release; is it to broadcast information, increase business, update your target users?
2. Who would you like to read the release?
3. Have you actually included information that will be of interest to the reader?
4. Is there a just cause for releasing the information you wish to broadcast; are you launching a new product or service, have you won an award, been contacted by aliens or had another exciting event happen that readers might be interested in?
5. What would you like to happen when people read the press release; book an appointment, order a product, telephone for more information or just pass it on to their friends?

So, now that you have decided what you are going to write about and why, you do need to ensure that it follows certain guidelines for layout and content:-

1. Please try to ensure that your writing is grammatically correct and doesn't contain any spelling mistakes or errors, and that any sources you have used are quoted correctly.
2. Do keep it to the point, and don't use unnecessary flowery language simply to fill a word count.
3. Ensure that what you say is true and correct and doesn't embellish anything with questionable statements or suggestions
4. Try to be objective, although I appreciate that this might be almost impossible to do.

5. Try to see your release through your customers eyes, what would they like to read? What might make them take it to the next stage? However, do remember the point above.

6. Try not to send out a release too early or too late. Try to keep it topical, especially if it keys into current news and affairs that readers may be interested in.

86. Tinyurl.com

You may have noticed whilst you were reading that a few of the web addresses I have used look unusual, if not downright odd. This is because the originating web addresses are too long and would be complex to type out.

In addition, if you have ever done anything at all with affiliate programmes, you may have been surprised to discover just how long some of the URL's (*uniform resource locators* or web addresses to you and me) can be for your links. They contain all sorts of symbols, and may even go on for more than one line. In some cases, they may not even fit in the place you would like them to go, because they are just too darned long.

TinyUrl is a handy little online service that converts long web addresses into nice, easy to write down short ones, which can then be posted into any email or website with confidence. Best of all it is free (but if you like it, and use it a lot you may want to donate some money to them because they are so helpful). Not only that, if you are using them for affiliate links they will also protect the original affiliate link from viewers, which means that someone has to follow the link to find out where it is going. Try it out by typing this web address into your browser to see where it takes you to ***http://tinyurl.com/39elty***. To find out more about making tiny web addresses, visit ***tinyurl.com*** and just try it out

87. E-junkie

You have the website, you have an e-book, some music, an image or some software you want to sell, and you may already be selling them on Ebay. But how will you deliver the product to your customer after they have purchased it? You may decide to create a new folder on your website that is not linked to anything else on the website (because you don't want the search engines to find it and index it), then store your new e-book, software, image or music in this folder.

When someone buys your e-book, you can send them a link to the e-book, image, software or music so that they can download it... moreover, so can anyone else if that person later forwards the link on! Hopefully, you can easily spot the possible pitfalls to such a method of delivering your digital goods.

Once the web address to your work is known it can be passed on to anyone else and they will be able to download it as well. This is where a really useful service called e-junkie comes in very useful indeed. It acts a bit like a secure vault that only allows access to the product after your customer has jumped a number of fences - usually confirming payment at the very least.

In brief, you create a payment link on your site (or in your ebay shop) to your product and when a customer completes payment they are automatically redirected to the right place to download it. It works with all the major payment processing systems such as paypal, google checkout and clickbank. As the download page is only available for a short period of time, it means that there is little or no opportunity for fraudulent activity. You can find e-junkie at this web address: ***www.ejunkie.com***

E-junkie does charge for the service, but prices start at just $5.00 (yes that's around £2.50) per month for up to ten items. You can use the service to sell all sorts of things from digital goods, like those mentioned above or tangible products such as CD's or even tickets for events. In fact it's a brilliant online shopping cart as well, that just happens to be tailored specifically for digital product delivery.

This is also time to mention that this is the very question the music industry has been banging on about for years; and believe me I now know how they feel! I have listed a number of other online services that provide a similar service to e-junkie on the website.

88. CD baby

No, this is not an online service for parents or children, rather it is a rather nifty little helper that provides the musicians amongst us with a platform to sell their own music. Yes, I know that you probably have your own myspace page, but surely you aren't relying solely on that are you?

CD Baby is one of a number of online services that provide the musician with a way to easily get their CD's and music tracks onto online databases like itunes, Raphsody and Yahoo! Music. When they sell one of your CD's, they keep $4.00 (yes this is another US service, but that shouldn't really matter in the online world) and pay you the rest of whatever you have set as your sales price. They will even provide you with UPC (unique product code) so that you can add your CD to Amazon if you want to. Of course, the service costs, you wouldn't expect it not to would you? But at only $35.00 (around £17.50) it has to be one of the best value services around. For that $35 they will set up a webpage just for your CD's, they add them to their databases, they process all the credit card info so you don't have to, and they email you every time you make a sale. In addition to everything listed so far, you also get the opportunity to allow your music to be sold via digital distribution, so it gets listed on all sorts of other music providers for free. Although they act as your distributor, you still retain rights over your music and are free to sell it where you will. But, one word of warning, if you have already signed up the same CD's with another distributor, don't add it to CD Baby as well or they will get confused.

89. Securing e-books

Let's assume that you have written a best selling e-book and you've used a standard word processor to write your tome. You now have the happy task of distributing it in a format that is suitable for the Internet. There are a number of things you need to be aware of when writing anything for distribution on the web:-

- Not everyone has MS Word on their computer. Yes, shock/horror, there are people that do not use, or like, Microsoft products!
- MS Word and other word processing software is not inherently secure and readers could cut and paste parts of the book into their own documents and try to pass it off as their own work.
- The way that a word-processed document prints out depends on the settings on the computer of the person that has purchased your book - and **NOT** the settings you created the original document with. At it's worst, this may mean that an index or content list may not match up with the page numbers that are printed.

For all these reasons, you need to find an easier, and more secure, distribution method.

The most commonly used method is to create a PDF (*portable document format*) version of the word processed document - in some word processors you can simply 'print' your book to a pdf version meaning you don't have to buy yet more expensive software. PDF files mean that your book is printed in the way in which YOU laid it out, and not according to the settings of your customers' computer.

However, one of the biggest advantages of PDF is that it also has basic security built in. You can make sure that people cannot select text (for cut and paste functions), they will not be able to edit the text and you can even add a password. However, it does mean that your customer needs to have a PDF reader on their computer although they normally come pre-loaded on new computers these days and if not, are usually free, (if you don't have one go to ***www.acrobat.com*** for theirs).

However, the use of PDF does not overcome one of the biggest potential headaches for e-book writers, which is that of forwarding the file onto friends, relatives and colleagues of the person that originally bought it. Now, you may or may not think that this is a huge problem, but if you do feel it is an issue or it becomes an issue in the future, then you need a way of securing your book so that only the person that bought it can read it. To create this sort of security you might use a piece of software that will provide a way of encrypting the book - in other words making it look like gobbledegook if the activation key for the encryption isn't on the same computer. There are too many to list in this short tip, but I have compiled a list of the available software, together with relevant links, on the website.

90. Google base

You may have noticed, Google is kind of the main kid on the block as far as many of the current methods for driving traffic to your website are concerned and it pays dividends to make sure that you are well listed on it, because it really can make or break a website. However, this pre-eminence may not always be the case and you can be sure I will always keep you up-to-date with new developments on the website. However, for the time being we will stick to the current 'leader of the pack'.

To submit your website to the Google database you can take a variety of approaches:

- You can simply wait for the Google spider to find you,
- you can submit your site to the Google spider,
- or, you can use Google Base.

The advantage of Google Base is that as well as letting it have information about your website, you can also submit offline content, such as a research paper you have written or the pictures you have just taken; you can submit information about events as I do for my seminars, personal ads, recipes, reviews or even information about yourself - if you are offering a service perhaps. You don't even need to have a website as Google will store documents for you and make them available to anyone that is looking for it through it's normal database.

When you have created an item on Google Base you then give it 'attributes' and labels, which are used to describe what it is. Labels are keywords and phrases that classify the item - such as product or website. Attributes are words and phrases which describe the characteristics and qualities of the item, for example if you are adding a website you might add its name, the audience it is intended for, whether it is about health or rearing guinea pigs, how many pages it has etc.... However, there is some debate about whether individual web pages are classed as individual items or are part of a whole. You will have to make a judgement yourself about whether to list individual pages or list the whole website as a single entity.

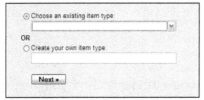 To submit an item you can either use the form that Google kindly provide, or you can use their 'bulk upload' feature if you have more than 10 'items' to include. Even if your website is already listed on Google, it may do even better in the search results as a result of using Google Base because you are adding more information about its relevancy - which is one of the most important attributes that Google has for any search result.

Once you have added all your information to Google Base, then it can be found on the Google search engine and on other Google services such as Google Maps. However, do bear in mind that if you have submitted an e-book, music track or photo to Google Base, then they may make it wholly available - in which case you might not be able to charge for it and people could view it free of charge. In this case you would need to use the PRODUCT attribute so that the database knows it is to be sold.

To use Google Base you will need an account with Google. However this can be the same account that you use for almost everything else that you do with Google (Adwords, Books or even Adsense). Click along to ***base.google.com*** and have a look at what there is in the way of information: then why not sign up and create your first item, if you have something to add already!

91. Online galleries

So far we have talked about authors and musicians, but perhaps you are a photographer, a graphic designer, an artist or an illustrator. Even if you aren't an artist, you may still be interested in this hint because this is where you can obtain good quality images, pictures or art for your book cover, your office or your shop.

I don't how you go about selling your work at present, but I bet that you at least display some in a gallery somewhere. Of course, the biggest problem with this is that the gallery has to get visitors through the door in the first place. You may even have a website, but this has a metaphorical door too and, as with any website, people need to know you are there.

What I am talking about are the various online markets that bring artists together with purchasers. There are two main types. The first is the classic gallery, but in an online sense. These deal with all sorts of artwork, from acrylics, to mosaics and ceramics. Typically, they will need to review your work before accepting it onto the gallery. Most artwork in such a gallery is for sale and the sales process may involve a number of steps before payment can be taken - this is because most artwork is unique, and the owner will need to confirm that it is still available before any sale takes place.

The second type of gallery is mainly for flat media artists, illustrators, photographers and graphic designers. These galleries provide stock images that people like me can buy for small amounts of money to use as book covers, t-shirt images and postcards. They are royalty free for the purchaser, which means that once they pay the required amount of money for the image, they are free to use it as they wish as long as they stick to the rules they have agreed to in their purchase. This benefits the creator as well since each image can be sold over and over again.

You can get some fantastic images for just one credit ($1) that could be used in your website logo. In fact, these services are where I source all the images I use as covers for my books, and they also feature in the design of a number of websites I own too.

If you are an artist then creating an account is normally free of charge in both cases; you can then add as many pieces of your work as you would like, in fact quantity works well. You set the prices you would like to charge - although there may be guidelines that you need to stick to. You also agree the royalty payments you would like to receive.

In order to use any of these services, you will need to list the images of your artwork using appropriate keywords or by assigning categories so that people can find them. It goes without saying of course that you do need to be the creator of the image that you are uploading otherwise you could be in a whole lot of trouble over copyright. For a list of services that you could use to promote your artwork, visit the resources section of the website where there is a handy list of links for you to explore.

92. Joint ventures

'Joint Ventures' is a term, usually used by Governments when they are seeking private funding for public initiatives (at least that is the case in the UK). As far as we are concerned though, it works in a very similar way, except that you *dear reader*, are hoping that someone who has a lot of experience in the field you are working in (in other words a *guru*) will allow you access to their mailing or membership list in return for a 'cut' of any sales you manage to make of your product or service.

The people who receive the email or contact from *'the guru'* will already be in the market for the product you are selling. They will probably have bought before, or at the very least they will have deliberately signed up to receive the emails they get; which all in all means that they are very good prospects indeed.

All YOU need to do is identify which one of the *guru's* that work in your field you would like to work with and then approach them with a request to help you with the marketing of your product, in return for a (generous) commission.

You will probably need to create a web page/site that has been customised for their particular mailing list; you may even find that you are given lots of ideas by your *guru* on how to make this an effective sales tool. You will also need to write an email or letter that is sufficiently enticing to encourage the mailing list recipients to follow the link embedded in it to your web page. It might also be a good idea to offer the respondents something free as well, in this way you can also begin to build your own mailing list - but do make it relevant and worth having, as you don't want to damage the reputation of your *guru* by offering something that isn't worth the electronic paper it is printed on!

Who sends the email to the list will be a matter for discussion between you and your *guru*, although usually the list owner does this part of the work. Who manages the web page is also up for discussion, although you may want to keep control of this element yourself. Don't forget to keep meticulous records of sales to share with your *guru*: this will demonstrate that you are being up-front about their earnings, and may well mean that they will be happy to work with you in the future.

93. Google books

Let's say you have become a world famous author, well maybe not quite world famous - but an author nevertheless. Unless you are a 'name' with a major publisher, you may find that your book languishes at the bottom of the sales lists. So how can you get your new book noticed? There are numerous things you could do to promote it, including selling it on Ebay, through Amazon Advantage or your own website (depending on any agreements you may have with your publishers of course). But let's say that you want people to be able to find it on the web, through a search engine like Google for instance, how might you do that?

Well you might choose to use Google Book Search. Google Book Search is one of the latest in a family of products that Google are producing to fulfil their mission statement "to organize the world's information and make it universally accessible and useful". Firstly any book you want to include needs to have an ISBN number (International Standard Book Number) which you can only get through a publisher, although you can self-publish as I have talked about earlier in the book.

You will then submit the book to Google, either as a physical copy or as a PDF file. They, in turn, will scan it and  make it available through their search engine.

"What about my copyright? And surely if someone can see my book they won't want to buy it anymore". This, of course, is where Google wizardry comes in. A user will only ever be able to see a tiny proportion of your book (in line with copyright allowances) and the bit that they see is related to the search terms they used in the first place. This should be just enough for them to decide if it is the right book for them. If it is, they can then click on one of the links presented which will take them to their choice of online marketplace. You can get more information about Google Book Search by going to ***books.google.com***. Interestingly, Amazon also have their own version of Google Book Search called Search Inside which works in a very similar way, and if you are registered with their Amazon Advantage programme you should be able to participate in the programme.

94. Amazon advantage

I suspect that the vast majority of people reading this book have used Amazon at some point to buy a book, CD or a DVD and in a sense, this is what Amazon Advantage is all about. It enables the small trader to utilise the power of this vast online shopping experience to sell our own books, CD's and DVD's. If you have written a book, produced your own DVD or CD and, as long as it has been published (and you can even do this yourself), you can have Amazon stock it on your behalf and then sell it with the powerful tag that all buyers see "ships in 24 hours".

Having said all that, it's not for the faint hearted; Amazon take a hefty slice as commission and they expect you to cover the costs of shipping their stock to them; and they only pay you when they have sold an item. However, in terms of reaching a wider audience for a product than you might otherwise; it is one that can't be beaten (for the moment at any rate).

Currently, one of the books I have listed in the UK Amazon Advantage programme stands as the number one result when you type '*hysterectomy*' into the search box, although this will be subject to change as more books are brought out by other authors and publishers. Joining is not quite free as there is an annual membership fee (2007 fees were £23.50 in the UK and $29.95 in the US) and you do need to make sure that your book, CD or DVD is in their catalogue as they won't be able to list it otherwise. Once you have filled out the application, you will normally be asked to ship one or two items to start with. Their automated system will arrange for more orders in the future depending on the levels of sales. This can be a bit hit and miss sometimes and I have been caught out occasionally when they have run out of stock unexpectedly and no longer display the 'ships within 24 hours' tag next to the books. To find out more why not head over to ***www.amazon.com/advantage***.

95. Adbrite

If you have an information website, let's say it's a site for your local community, then you may be looking to advertising as your main source of revenue. However, as we have already considered earlier in the book, running your own advertising programme is not an easy business, and this is where an aggregated service such as Adbrite might be able to help.

Adbrite (**www.adbrite.com**) is an online marketplace that manages supply and demand for adverts. It joins those who want to advertise on the Internet with those who want to make some money by displaying those adverts. It started in 2002, which in web terms is probably the equivalent of three or four decades of success. Individuals, websites and companies can place targeted adverts across a huge number of sites. You get to choose the type of site, the context, type of user and even the type of ad (banner, text or whole pages). Webmasters looking to improve their advertising income can choose which sorts of adverts they will use, whose adverts to show and they can even customise them so that they fit in seamlessly with the look and feel of their site.

Website owners get to set the rates for their sites and can also provide an additional income stream to their visitors who may just be in the market for an advert themselves, through the Adbrite referral programme. Fortunately, the Adbrite ads will also work in conjunction with Google Adsense, meaning that you can increase the advertising revenue beyond the maximum number of displays that Adsense sets.

The types of ads you can display are the ubiquitous banners (which are fully customisable) and text ads. There is also the option to use something called interstitials, which are full-page interactive ads containing an advertisers landing page or branding message. They usually appear in the main window after a visitors third page view. If you don't really follow how this might affect your own site, have a look at the Adbrite demo site to get a feel: you can find it on their website.

The Instant Business Opportunity

Edgar was full of brilliant ideas that would make millions
by lunchtime tomorrow!
© Photographer: Dejan Savic | Agency: Dreamstime.com

Are you good at marketing? Do you have an eye for an advert?
Could you sell coal to a miner, ice to the Inuit, sand to a
Bedouin? If the answer to any of these questions is **YES**, then
you may well be ripe for any one of a number of ready-made
online businesses that have been set up to make life easier for
the eager entrepreneur. Sure, the returns aren't as good as they
might be if you did it all yourself, but the advantage is the
owners have already worked out what is successful, what is not
and you don't have to go through that huge learning curve. To
succeed you need to be able to apply yourself in the area of
marketing and selling. It takes commitment and time, but the
rewards can be substantial.

96. CB mall

CB Mall stands for ClickBank Mall and it is a fantastic tool that you can use to promote all the products that are available on ClickBank. I have already talked about ClickBank itself earlier in the book, but in brief, it is an online market place where you can buy some of the best digital goods that the Internet has to offer, whether this is software or an e-book. If you haven't visited it yet, why not do so now - you won't regret it at all.

CB Mall takes the ClickBank market-place and enables you to promote the entire ClickBank database with simple, easy marketing techniques that encourage people to visit the site. Almost everything sold through your link to CB Mall will result in affiliate earnings for you, with the exception of a small number of banner ads. Therefore, if you have a ready-made audience then adding CB Mall to your website could be one of the easiest ways to supplement your income. You can find it yourself at *www.cbmall.com*. You can also see it in action on the Grow A Better Business website.

97. Chat rooms

There are a million and one opportunities to run a chat room (oh alright, I may be exaggerating a little here, but it certainly feels like there are this number when you are searching out the opportunities!). One of the advantages of a hosted chat room is that you don't have to do any of the programming or even build the website because that is all taken care of by the owners. All you have to do is promote the site and collect the money from people signing up to it. We have chat rooms for book lovers, chat rooms for dating, chat rooms for friends, chat rooms for the holistic community - in fact just about any subject you can think of will have a chat room available for you to promote if you want to.

98. Free dating sites

Let's use diy-dating (*tinyurl.com/29txgo*) as an example - you can find some links to get you started in the resources section of the website. To get started you simply set up a **FREE** account; it is commission based and your earnings are based on receiving a percentage of the fees paid whenever someone upgrades their membership. Your site is created for you, free of charge, and your statistics show that you already have 100's of thousands of members, which gives your new potential members lots of opportunities to find the mate of their dreams. They offer a huge range of templates if you are going for a simple stand-alone website, or you have the opportunity to integrate the look with any other website you might own. Because the 'back end' system handles the transactions, all you have to do is concentrate on your sites' look, feel and the marketing - see what I mean about being good at marketing!

So in very simple terms:
- You create an account with your supplier
- You create your first website
- They maintain the website for you and make sure that there are already lots of people for your new members to choose from
- You send lots of people along to join it!

Let's think about how you might market it though!
- You could put an advert in the local press

- You could add it to your current website - if it's appropriate to do so
- You could put a leaflet through every door in your local community
- You could have stickers made up for your car
- You could tell all your friends, relations and work colleagues about your new site
- You could have some business cards created and agree to leave them at the local pub
- You could use Google Adwords
- You could create a viral marketing campaign

There are so many things you could do to promote your new site and I am sure you will come up with another dozen to add to those I have added here. The only thing that limits this sort of opportunity is your imagination and ingenuity for selling.

99. Become an ISP

If your business is related to anything 'Internet' such as web design then you might like to think about becoming an Internet Service Provider (ISP) by using one of the many reseller accounts that are available. As with many other similar business offerings, your role as a reseller is simply to market the product and gather in your new customers. In some cases you set the fees that are charged, in others the fees are standard and set by the original host. Usually you can create custom packages that have a variety of services attached to them for different sorts of customer.

The advantage of being a reseller, especially if you are a web designer, is that you can add hosting to your list of services. Alternatively, you could throw in hosting as part of the overall cost, if you wanted to make your services particularly attractive to any potential customers.

100. Cafepress.com

Cafepress is a great add-on for an existing website, particularly those that have a community attached to them. It is free to sign up and you can give it a look and feel that matches your main site. It allows you to sell a range of merchandise including tee shirts, hats, jumpers, mugs and even mouse mats. You could even customise the merchandise you sell with your own logos, images, brands and trademarks. When you do this, other people with Cafepress shops are also able to sell your products as well.

This is one of those fantastic ways to increase a feeling of inclusiveness for your community - whether it is a local dating site (badges might be good for blind daters to help identify each other in a crowded bar) to a local charity for children - and everything in between of course. You can find it at **www.cafepress.com**

101. The last one

As my last hint for building a brilliant business with the Internet, I thought I would share with you a few of the techniques that I have used to ensure that The Hysterectomy Association remains one of the top sites for women's health in the UK and abroad. Taking a step by step approach, I will explain how the whole thing hangs together and how it makes money:-

1. Website

- This is full of information in the form of individual information pages
- I add news about current research and trends to the site, which helps to keep it fresh and ensures that the website is visited regularly by the search engine spiders.
- I have provided a discussion forum, which has several thousand members and tens of thousands of messages listed. This encourages people to engage with each other, provides a lot of support and extra information creating a genuine online community.

2. Marketing

- I place adverts on Google Adwords, Yahoo! Search Marketing and Microsoft AdCenter, which all point to specific pages on the main website
- I write articles about relevant women's health topics and I regularly add to the hysterectomy topic on wikipedia, including a link back to the site

- Every website I create has a link to the hysterectomy association
- At the end of the free booklet (a short e-book) there is a poster that will also be printed out, I encourage readers to give this to their GP surgery or local hospital
- I am regularly contacted by journalists who are looking for information and/or case studies. I always ensure that they will mention the site in their article. Because of the power of my mailing list, I can ensure several hundred responses in just a couple of hours.
- I have created two sets of emails that people can subscribe to; the first is for those who have yet to have their surgery, and the second provides recovery information. Each email is full of useful information and includes a strong call to action, either to visit the site or to make a purchase.
- I send out a monthly newsletter to all the people on my mailing list with the latest information from the website as well as introducing one of our products
- I add a link to the website every time I make a relevant posting somewhere on the web and I also provide links back to other sites with complementary information or services.

3. **Monetizing the Site**

- I display Adsense on the forums and on some information pages on the main website
- I have adverts for our own products on the site as well to ensure that people are reminded that these products exist.
- I also promote a number of compatible products from other providers

- I sell three of my own books, two books by another author and an e-book by my husband John. I also sell tummy support products which help during recovery.
- I have listed the e-book version of my books on clickbank. I also have a separate website called **your-hysterectomy.com** where I sell all the e-books in a single document called The Complete Guide To Hysterectomy.
- I supply two of my books to Amazon UK through it's advantage programme
- I have also published three of the books through Lulu, which enables them to be listed on Amazon in the United States as well.
- Finally, I also list the books on ebay, on payloadz and other digital marketplaces.

Hopefully the list above will give you some ideas about how you can bring everything I have talked about in the book together to build your brilliant business online.

Well that's it for this book. Please feel free to email me at linda@growabetterbusiness.co.uk if you want to ask a question or if you want to make a comment and I always appreciate feedback, if you feel like sending me some.

　　　If you are local to Dorset, then you might be interested in the workshops and mentoring services I offer and you can find out more on my website at: www.growabetterbusiness.co.uk

Good Luck.

Linda

www.ingramcontent.com/pod-product-compliance
Lightning Source LLC
Chambersburg PA
CBHW021142070326
40689CB00043B/961